BRIDGES

LEADERS CONNECTING PEOPLE TO PURPOSE

JOHNATHAN WILLIAMS

Title: BRIDGES – Leaders Connecting People to Purpose

Author: Johnathan Williams

I0833771

Publishing Consultant: Lakeya Tucker, www.mltconsulting.net

Editor: Monick, @Monick_edit

ISBN No: 979-8-218-91571-1

Contact Information: Johnathan Williams, jwdocumentmanagement@gmail.com

Contents

Acknowledgements

I didn't arrive here by myself. Just like bridges carry others, I have experienced those who carried me through some of my toughest seasons and my highest achievements. They shared in my struggles, the tensions, the celebrations, and even the doubts. This is an acknowledgement of those who quietly influenced and groomed me, often without even realizing it.

Some of my closest friends and former friends taught me many great lessons. My peers showed me the power of struggle and necessity of perseverance. My colleagues and partners imparted their wisdom through word and deed, which led to the inspiration for this book.

To those who led with integrity, who were consistent in their approach, and who handled me with grace and intentionality, this book stands on the pillars you helped build. To you do I tip my hat and give gratitude. Attempting to list the name of every influence would only prolong this section, but to those who read this and recall your placement in my life in the past or the present, please know that there are not enough words to express my gratefulness and thankfulness for you.

Introduction

Perception is Reality

In leadership, and just as in life, we are all building something. We're building a structure that either stands under pressure or collapses under its own weight. Some of us are still laying the foundation, and others are already spanning great distances, but no matter where you are on that journey, there are three pillars that will determine the strength of your structure. Every leader and every individual striving for excellence must learn to manage three major things**.** **Perception, Professionalism**, and **Productivity**.

I call them the Three P's, and they have quietly guided every decision, every season of growth, and every leadership lesson in my life. Whether I was in the military, corporate boardrooms, or consulting for organizations trying to find their balance again, these three principles have remained constant. They've shaped how I show up, how I'm perceived, and how I continue to evolve.

These are the guardrails that shape how we are seen, how we show up, and how we sustain success.

1. Perception – Perception is reality. However, it's not always truth, but it is always powerful. The way people see you, your attitude, your work ethic, your tone, and your presence often

determine the doors that open or close in your career. You can't control every narrative about you, but you can influence the story by managing how you are perceived. Managing perception isn't manipulation, but I would call it stewardship. It's about making sure your intentions and your impact align - which is the hardest thing we can do in any type of relationship. Your quality of work, your consistency, and your character should all speak the same language. Over time, those elements create the perception of who you are as a professional and as a person.

One of the best tools you can have as a leader is the tool of understanding. In my years of experience across industries, serving different leaders, and navigating teams of varying ages, ethnicities, and backgrounds, I've learned that the impact of my influence is either propelled by or limited by my ability to understand people and their emotions. That lesson has been tested repeatedly, and it has never failed to prove true.

The ability to apply proper management techniques of emotional intelligence is a skill that is unmatched and second to none. What people perceive is directly tied to how you make them feel. Emotional intelligence is not just a buzzword; it's a muscle that can be developed over time. The key to mastering it lies in learning to see and think objectively when engaging with others, while also having the foresight to understand how your words and actions today will affect relationships tomorrow.

The great news is that this skill isn't new. It's rooted in something we've all practiced since childhood—relationship building. As we grow older, we often forget or mishandle this simple technique, but just as with any structure, leadership requires connection points. Influence is sustained through relationships, and the best way to understand someone is to know them well enough to anticipate how they will respond to your message, no matter how heavy your words may be. As the saying goes, your reputation will precede you.

Managing perception doesn't mean pretending or performing, but it does mean being intentional about the message of your work, your energy, and your character in every room you enter. It is often shaped by two things: the quality of your work and the consistency of your conduct. When you deliver excellence consistently, people begin to associate your name with reliability and dependability. When your words match your actions, people begin to trust your integrity. This is how we begin to build our professional brand and reputation.

In this way, perception becomes less about optics and more about authenticity, which is something we strive to have in every area of our lives. The focus then becomes about earning and cultivating a reputation that reflects the truth of who you are and the standard you live by. When we learn to build relationships rooted in understanding, our perception begins to align with our reality. People no longer just see what you do; they begin to feel who you are.

2. Professionalism – If perception is the story others tell about you, then we can view professionalism as the story you tell about yourself. It's how you present and carry your personal brand in every interaction, no matter whether you're speaking to an executive, a peer, or a customer. However, professionalism is unique in that it is both visible and invisible. It

shows up in your appearance, your punctuality, and your posture, but it also lives in your tone, your disposition, and the quiet way you respect others even when you disagree with them.

True professionalism means that your presentation and your principles are not only in lockstep, but they are in harmony. They complement each other. You don't compromise your character to be liked or your ethics to be promoted and applauded. You take responsibility for your words, your decisions, and your impact, and this is the alignment that transforms professionalism from a checklist or a common corporate principle into a form of leadership that is loud even when you haven't spoken a word. It's not just about how you look at work, but it's really about how you lead, even when no one is watching.

3. Productivity - Productivity, although mentioned last, is what completes the cycle. Your perception and professionalism set the tone and stage, but your productivity delivers proof of who you are. The quality and consistency of your output determine whether your reputation grows, stagnates, or declines. Productivity is not just about doing more to be seen, but it's about doing

what matters, doing it well, and doing it with intense purpose.

When productivity is grounded in professionalism, your work carries the weight of your intensity. When productivity is supported by perception, your results speak for themselves, and you never have to say a word. In this way, each of the three P's reinforces the concept of the others:

- Perception determines how your work is received.
- Professionalism determines how your work is respected.
- Productivity determines how your work is remembered.

Together, they create a cycle of credibility. Your productivity fuels your reputation, your professionalism sustains it, and your perception amplifies it. When you learn to manage all three with intention, you don't put on a performance; you lead. When you show up in any space, you aren't just present, but you carry presence. As we move through the rest of this book, you'll see how these same principles show up in different bridge types.

The goal of writing this book is to help you incorporate the Three P's into your leadership style. The goal is also to challenge your idea of leadership, create an opportunity to evaluate your approach to collaboration, invite questions about how you view and approach your team's success, and challenge you to develop, create, and strengthen your roles within your environment. If you desire to explore these areas or have not often considered these ideas, just know you have a partner while exploring these principles, self-assessing your individual effectiveness, embracing the ideologies described herein, and sifting through the actions that must be taken to build an effective and cohesive team.

Passage and Purpose

Throughout history, bridges have served one sacred function: passage. Not just across rivers or valleys, but between possibilities. Between people. Between moments of survival and seasons of thriving. Bridges have always been more than stone and steel. They are statements of intent; declarations that something worth connecting lies on the other side.

Bridges can come in many different shapes, sizes, and designs. Their locations may vary, but their purpose remains the same: connecting people and resources together and overcoming obstacles that are seemingly impassable or uncrossable. They were used, and still are used, to provide access between regions, cities, goods, and essential services. The obstacles that bridges can be built over may vary as well. Roadways, railways, bodies of water, valleys, mountainous terrain; all of these things can impede the way of life that we try to create for ourselves.

Despite location, design complexity, or the need for a bridge, they share a common thread: bridges are built out of necessity. A bridge is built because of a need, not a luxury. The use and construction of bridges can be found as far back as 1300 BC during the Mycenaean period. Specifically, the Arkadiko Bridge was originally built for chariot passage and is the oldest known dateable bridge in the world. Some of the earliest known bridges in existence are the Caravan Bridge in Turkey and the Tarr Steps in England.

Despite their age and lack of modern materials, these bridges are *still* in use today! Even after being damaged by floods, wind, and rain, these bridges have been repaired, restored, and rebuilt to continue serving their nearby communities. Many of the bridges built during this time were built using masonry stones, limestone boulders, and small pieces of tile, tightly packed together with little to no mortar. Civil engineers and construction gurus of today would scoff at the construction and design of bridges in the olden days.

Despite their lack of visual appeal and wonder, these bridges served as early designs for future builders throughout world history, and some have withstood the test of time.

As we have progressed as a society and faced various changes throughout history, our designs and understanding of the need for bridges have birthed ingenuity and creativity into our land. We no longer depend on horse-drawn carriages and chariots to move our resources and families. As our society evolved, so did our need to create faster means of ground transportation.

Hence, the birth of trains and automobiles of all sizes. No matter how fast our vehicles became, we still faced the impenetrable stare of natural obstacles and impasses, which continued the need for larger, longer, and taller bridges.

Just as bridges connect physical locations, leaders connect people, ideas, and resources. They also close the gaps in understanding, helping to navigate challenging situations, and building pathways to success. Like the engineers who design and construct bridges, leaders must possess vision, strategic thinking, and the ability to adapt to changing circumstances. The principles of bridge building – strength, stability, adaptability – are also the cornerstones of effective leadership.

Just as there is a bridge for most terrain, there is a leadership style for every challenge. Every influential leader must first understand the landscape they're bridging, what divides and exists between their people and their purpose. What terrain is impassable unless someone dares to lay down the beams, cables, and arches of support, strategy, and compassion.

The evolution of bridge designs is a direct reflection of the builder's understanding of not only short-term needs, but also a deeper understanding of the need for diverse approaches to challenges that the community at large will face. A simple beam bridge might suffice for a short span, while a complex suspension bridge is necessary for crossing vast distances. Similarly, in the realm of leadership, different situations call for different approaches. Simply stated, effective leaders must be able to adapt their style to the specific needs of their team and the challenges they face.

Comparatively, leadership styles also serve a purpose, and the correct application of a leadership style can change the trajectory of someone's life, the direction of an organization, provide access to critical resources, and impact the effectiveness of a ministry. History shows us that different challenges require different approaches, and the ability to recognize the best approach in critical situations is just as important as solving the problem itself. Fortunately, or unfortunately, true leadership is a skill that is learned, and rarely an innate skillset.

In scripture, passage is often marked by crossing — the Red Sea, the Jordan River, the road to Damascus. In each crossing, there is not just movement, there is intention. What lay ahead wasn't just another place; but there was destiny in the distance. It was purpose revealed through passage.

Likewise, when a leader builds a bridge, organizationally, relationally, spiritually, they are not just solving a problem. They are aligning someone with a greater calling. Purpose is not a destination; it is the unfolding of alignment with an original and intentional design, and every bridge is a chance to step closer to it.

There are seven main types of bridges that we use today, and they can be directly correlated to leadership styles, which we will discover together over the next few chapters.

1. The Arch Bridge – The Servant Leader. The arch is rooted in strength through humility. Like servant leaders, the arch redistributes pressure away from itself to support the whole structure. It is ancient, tested, and resilient. Their strength is in their humility and their quiet reliability.
   - Perception: Often seen as dependable and selfless but can be overlooked or underestimated if they don't communicate their value.

- Professionalism: Expressed through consistency, character, and commitment to service; tends to lead by example rather than authority.
- Productivity: High and steady; results are built on long-term trust and stability rather than speed or flash

Lesson: Servant leaders must learn to let their strength be seen for influence, not for ego.

2. The Beam Bridge – The Transactional Leader. Straightforward, foundational, and reliable. Beam bridges represent leaders who create clear expectations and deliver on them, often in straightforward, rule-bound environments. They provide structure and predictability in uncertain times.
    - Perception: Viewed as stable, trustworthy, and efficient, but may be perceived as rigid or uninspired if they resist new ideas.
    - Professionalism: Defined by fairness, punctuality, and adherence to process. They bring discipline where chaos might otherwise reign.
    - Productivity: Reliable and consistent, though sometimes lacking innovation

when systems become the focus instead of people.

Lesson: Transactional leaders must remember that structure should serve people, not replace connection.

3. The Cantilever Bridge – The Strategic Leader. These bridges balance parts that project outward, requiring careful counterweights, just like leaders who think long-term, leveraging risk and reward with foresight and control. These leaders build from a firm base but aren't afraid to reach.
   - Perception: Seen as bold, innovative, and forward-thinking, but sometimes misunderstood as detached or idealistic.
   - Professionalism: Expressed through strategic foresight and conviction; professionalism means keeping vision and execution aligned.
   - Productivity**:** Fueled by creativity and purpose but requires grounding to ensure that vision doesn't outpace reality.

Lesson**:** Strategic leaders must anchor their reach in relationships, or they risk building in midair.

4. The Cable-Stayed Bridge – Collaborative Leaders. This bridge balances elegance with strength, much like transformational leaders

who lift the organization by providing strong values and vision. The central tower empowers the cables, just like a transformational leader empowers their team. These leaders thrive in team environments and believe in shared success.

- Perception: Seen as inclusive, empowering, and fair-minded, but can be perceived as overly democratic when decisive leadership is needed.
- Professionalism: Built on shared accountability and respect; they embody professionalism by creating psychological safety and shared ownership.
- Productivity: Strong when supported by team alignment; vulnerable when collaboration becomes consensus without direction.

Lesson: Collaborative leaders must learn when to listen and when to lead.

5. The Suspension Bridge – The Visionary/Empathetic Leader. Built for distance and flexibility, this bridge type symbolizes leaders who operate with high-level vision, able to flex across time, culture, and change while

maintaining a strong anchoring system. This leader thrives on connection and emotional intelligence.

- Perception: Warm, approachable, and emotionally aware; but if boundaries are unclear, they may be perceived as indecisive.
- Professionalism: Shown through empathy, understanding, and relational harmony. They maintain professionalism through compassion, not control.
- Productivity**:** At its best when the leader feels emotionally centered; too much emotional absorption can slow decision-making.

Lesson: Empathic leaders must balance compassion with clarity. It's ok to care deeply but lead firmly.

6. The Tied-Arch Bridge – The Transformational Leader. The tension in a tied-arch bridge is resolved through internal cooperation, just like leaders who rely on input and unity to keep the structure from collapsing. Strength comes from integration, not isolation, symbolizing a leader who bridges vision and reality, heart and head.

- Perception: Seen as inspiring and driven, often able to connect diverse groups toward a shared goal.
- Professionalism: Embodied through authenticity and courage; they elevate others by aligning purpose with performance.
- Productivity**:** Dynamic and high-impact, though sometimes inconsistent if energy isn't sustained by clear systems.

Lesson: Transformational leaders must ground inspiration in discipline to ensure that vision becomes legacy.

7. The Truss Bridge – The Structured Leader. Truss bridges adapt well to varied conditions by using interconnected triangles, similar to situational leaders who adjust their style based on the needs of their team, environment, or task. High strength through flexibility and structure. This leader excels in systems, detail, and execution.
    - Perception: Viewed as dependable, logical, and disciplined, but may be seen as inflexible or overly technical.
    - Professionalism: Evident through organization, reliability, and accountability. They bring structure to chaos and order to complexity.

- Productivity**:** Exceptionally high, though sometimes achieved at the expense of creativity or emotional connection.

Lesson: Structured leaders must remember that people are not parts; they're partners in the process.

You are not just called to build something; you are called to become the bridge. The one who carries people from confusion to clarity, from pain to purpose, from stagnation to movement. And just like any bridge, your strength won't come from perfection. It will come from your design, your intention, and your foundation in the One who already carried you across.

Consider what type of leader you are, and which bridges you most closely align with. Does your style of leadership work in your current environment? Each bridge is not just a structure; it's a metaphor for a moment. A moment when a leader decides to connect rather than separate and to serve rather than dominate. This is the passage that leads to purpose.

Every bridge has a purpose, and every leader has a structure. The strength of the structure depends on how well it manages weight, distributes tension, and adapts to change. The same is true for leadership. The Three P's act as universal forces that shape every bridge type differently. Your leadership style determines how you perceive yourself, how others perceive you, and how you respond under pressure. Understanding these differences helps you identify your natural design and strengthen it where it's weakest.

Chapter 1- The Arch Bridge

The Servant Leader

The Arch Bridge is one of the oldest and most reliable forms of infrastructure. Found as far back as ancient Mesopotamia, its defining feature is its curved design, which allows it to naturally transfer weight and pressure from the center of the arch (the keystone) outward and downward into its foundations.

Sydney Harbour Bridge https://www.australiantraveller.com/nsw/sydney/sydney-harbour-bridge/

One of the most easily recognizable and iconic Arch Bridges in the world is the Sydney Harbour Bridge, located in Australia. It is the largest steel arch bridge in the world. Before the bridge was constructed, Sydney was split into two sections—the north side, with about 300,000 residents, and the south side, which housed the central business district and about 600,000 people. As the population grew, there was an obvious need for something better than ferry travel across the harbor, which was often foggy and dangerous.

The need for a bridge to connect and unite Sydney was not born out of convenience, but from an overwhelming desire to connect almost 1 million people to resources that were otherwise limited, thereby increasing economic impact and creating stability throughout Sydney. More than 1,600 people worked on the bridge during its construction in 1923, and in 2017, more than 200 trains, 160,000 vehicles, and 1,900 bikes used the bridge every day. However well-intended, the construction of the bridge came with a cost, not just a financial one. Lives were lost, and families were shattered. Sixteen men were killed during the construction, often times from slipping off steel girders and plummeting into the cold, deep waters below.

Looking at the history of the Sydney Harbour Bridge, we can see that the cost of servitude and leadership for the greater good is often *sacrifice*. Sacrifices of time that could be spent engaging in self-serving activities, resources that would otherwise be used to benefit ourselves, and energy that could be devoted to building things in our personal lives. In many cases, all three of these sacrifices impact our families. Time is taken away from being present and available; resources that could be used to fortify the household; energy that could be used to enrich and gird the family dynamic. In extreme cases, we sometimes must sacrifice our very lives and livelihoods to serve and lead others.

Army 101

I'm reminded of my service in the Army Ordnance Corps and how I learned so much about how to lead by being thrust into a position of leadership. During the first few weeks of basic training, the drill sergeants would establish a clear hierarchy of leadership. But not long after week **1,** they would engage in creating an environment of trust by exercising "student leadership." Trainees would be designated as squad leaders or platoon guides (PG), and the goal was to have someone responsible for basic duties like accountability, marching the platoon, etc. Squad leaders were often rotated frequently and were tasked with passing on orders, assigning duties, and maintaining order within their squads.

From the position of Drill Sergeant, it was an opportunity to observe the strengths and weaknesses of those placed in those roles. My counterparts were all E2–E4, boasting experience in the workforce that should have mentally prepared them to navigate stressful territories or education that should have provided the agility and nimbleness to think critically in high-pressure environments. They tried their best to shine, but alas, they were quickly removed from those positions.

When my name was called on day eight to become a PG, I was a Private (E-1) who came from a National Guard unit in Macon, Georgia. I didn't have any formal college education or a robust work history to brag about, but I did have confidence. What I had in abundance was a disposition of fortitude and perseverance. The round I had in my chamber was life experience; a belief that no matter how low I was on the totem pole, I could become an influential and impactful leader, despite my perceived inexperience. This realization became a propelling force for me.

Within 2 days, I had proven that I knew how to march (thanks to my Sergeants back home), how to call cadences in step, sound off, and flow down clear guidance from our leadership team, and inspire others to follow even me, the least of the group. Proving this to others helped to show me my strengths and weaknesses, and it also introduced me to one of the most essential Army Values: Selfless Service. Leadership is not about having power; it is about wielding influence, sharing inspiration, building trust, and rallying and supporting a group of people to meet a shared goal. Being exposed to and learning the foundations of leadership in that space is what propelled me to where I am today.

In my current role, I came into this job knowing that challenges already existed. Confidence and trust in leadership had been eroded, and communication was siloed and almost nonexistent. There was no camaraderie or stability in the workforce, and processes were not established or clear across the team. These are challenges that many leaders face but rarely speak about. Leading people will always be more important than managing tasks, in my opinion. This is where the catalyst of change in someone else's life could begin. How we lead today will shape the perspective and influence the mentality of our teammates tomorrow.

However costly, the benefits of Arch-type leadership are plentiful, sustainable, impactful, and far-reaching, expanding across generations.

- Arch bridges are known for their durability and long-term reliability. In leadership, this translates to leaders who are consistent and unwavering. They are able to withstand storms that come and the pressure of leadership without crumbling. I would identify this leader's characteristic as "*Dependable*." They are resolute in their core beliefs and values. They are dutiful and are committed to seeing things through, even if it doesn't benefit them in the end.
- Arch bridges, because of how they are designed, naturally redistribute the weight of the bridge to its pillars. They bear heavy loads through compression rather than tension. I would identify this leader characteristic as "*Supportive*." They absorb the burden others cannot carry, offering safety and support, regardless of how heavy it may be. Not simply by carrying everyone and everything alone, but by

strategically redistributing pressure so the team can function.

- Arch bridges have a wedge-shaped stone placed at the very apex of the arch, called a "keystone." This stone is the final piece placed during construction, and it is the key element that locks all other stones into position, allowing the arch to support itself and any loads above. When translated to leadership, it is the equivalent of a "*Connector*" or "*Unifier*". Leaders who have this characteristic understand how people, ideas, and systems connect. They are relationship builders who align others around a shared purpose, ensuring everyone fits together.
- Arch bridges have many defining characteristics that make them different from other types of bridges. However, unlike other bridge types, the strength of the arch is in its shape, not its elevation. The shape…not its height; simply, the uniqueness of its design. What does this tell us about leadership? It shows us that leaders should focus more on their influence than on the spotlight. Arch leaders don't seek the attention or the credit, but their influence is often felt more than seen. They lead from beneath or from behind through service, not status—providing unseen, and often overlooked, strength that others stand on. Does this sound familiar? If not, it's called "*humility.*"

An arch bridge-style leader is a servant, stabilizer, and strength giver. They lead with quiet conviction, are built for endurance, and provide the foundational support others need to walk into their purpose. As a reminder, as a leader with this type of leadership style, you have to be careful to avoid burnout. We are not infallible, just mere mortals that have limits. Nevertheless, we can find multiple examples of this leadership style throughout world history if we look closely enough.

Harriet Tubman is often touted as a liberator, but if we compare her works to the arch bridge, we find that Tubman quietly and courageously supported others' liberation at great personal risk. She didn't seek power; she provided safe passage. Her strength was in how she anchored others and led them across impossible barriers. She was the bridge the Freedom Express needed to pass along the Underground Railroad.

Another example of arch bridge leadership is Mahatma Gandhi. Gandhi's leadership wasn't loud, but it was morally grounded and enduring. His ability to absorb opposition and redirect pressure nonviolently, without harm to his cause or his supporters, reflects the arch's ability to hold weight without collapse. His leadership was a forceful presence through peaceful and humble resistance.

But the best example we can always look to for this leadership style was Jesus Christ. His leadership was rooted in humility, sacrifice, and an unwavering commitment to uplifting others. Often revered as "the ultimate servant leader," Jesus bore the weight of others' burdens, served without seeking recognition, and became the keystone between humanity and God. He literally became the "connector" between Heaven and Earth, at the cost of his own life. There's no greater testament to the importance of cultivating these traits as leaders.

Each of these leaders didn't seek to stand above others; they chose instead to stand beneath them, quietly anchoring the weight of entire movements, communities, and moments in history. They became the strength others could stand on; the structure others could walk across. Through their endurance, they absorbed pressure so others could press forward. And through their faithfulness, they became living pathways that guided people through the dangerous, uncertain terrain of fear, oppression, doubt, and division.

Chapter 2- The Beam Bridge

The Transactional Leader

The Beam Bridge is the oldest of all bridge designs and one of the simplest. It is not particularly known for its elaborate (not so much) design or any eye-catching architecture, but it is recognized as the most functional and direct bridge type. Throughout its history, the beam bridge has been known for its simplicity. It is easy to design and requires fewer materials to construct than other types of bridges.

Lake Pontchartrain Causeway https://volkert.com/ projects/lake-pontchartrain-causeway/

The Lake Pontchartrain Causeway in southeastern Louisiana is among the longest overwater bridges in the world and holds the title as the longest bridge in the United States, spanning almost 24 miles. The original bridge was completed in 1956, and its twin was completed in 1969. As with most bridges, the bridge was constructed to provide a direct connection across an immovable obstacle in Lake Pontchartrain, which limited access from the north of New Orleans.

This type of leader has a reputation for being direct and straight to the point, but sometimes those traits can be misunderstood or land differently with each person they encounter. This leader may struggle to connect with others beyond task-based leadership. They are associated with being managers rather than mentors. Often lacking the influence of other leader types because of the personality type usually associated with Beam Leaders.

If you associate with this leadership style, you may have heard feedback that describes you as transactional by nature or motivated more by results rather than by relationships. This can lead to team members feeling undervalued due to the lack of connection. Be careful not to be inflexible. When receiving criticism, you may find yourself being resistant to change that requires you to shift your operational work style. This rigid structure will not work in environments that call for a high degree of emotional intelligence.

However damning that sounds, this leadership style has positive impacts. When properly prepared and self-aware, the Beam Leader is very dependable. They can become the backbone of day-to-day operational execution and clearly demonstrate the ability to achieve results through straightforward, practical approaches. If you're looking for efficiency, this leadership style often maintains timelines, systems, and processes in a way that helps others deliver work more effectively.

Rock, Paper, Scissors!

In 2024, I was doing a speaking engagement for students at Miami-Dade College titled "Embracing Authenticity and Personal Branding," intended for those preparing to enter the workforce and be confident and impactful. I opened with an ice breaker with the audience. It was a very familiar game called "Rock, Paper, Scissors". I called nine people up to participate in a fast-paced gauntlet to see who would win, and they worked through those rounds feverishly! It's amazing how people come alive when there's nothing to gain or lose, but they can just "be," without judgment.

During the game, the winners realized that they ended up with one of the three items: Rock, Paper, or Scissors. I let them (and my partners who were present) in on a secret: I analyze the patterns, words, and perspectives of my teammates, business partners, and friends to classify them as one of those items. Initially, they looked confused, but as I continued, it became clearer. Using the strengths and weaknesses of each item, I explained how this simple game helps categorize personality and working styles, ultimately helping us identify our authentic selves and determine what type of leader we might be or become. Remember: Paper covers rock, rock breaks scissors, and scissors cuts paper.

Sturdy Rock

We've all seen, held, or thrown a rock at some point in our lives. Rocks are naturally indifferent, being neither good nor bad in their nature. However, based on how we use them, they can be great additions to an environment or become the greatest obstacle you wish you never had. If you throw a rock into water, it hits hard, it sinks fast, it creates a splash, and then it's gone. That's how some rock-type leaders operate when their strength is mishandled. They try to lead with force, without strategy or awareness of the impact they have, be it positive or negative. They enter situations with brute authority, causing waves, unintentionally silencing voices, and driving ideas or people down.

However, if you skip a rock across water, something else happens. The surface tension of the water causes the rock to touch down just enough to move the water, lifting the rock and creating ripples that extend far beyond the point of impact. That's what a refined rock does. It knows when to apply pressure and when to pull back. The Rock leadership isn't a splash; it's a series of purposeful touches that move people forward without dragging them down. What am I saying here? The same personality style can be used to either create ripples of progress or completely sink relationships and stop momentum. Not all rocks have the same kind of impact; it just depends on how they're handled.

Rocks are innately solid and dense objects, and normally connected to traits like endurance, stability, or being immovable/stubborn. When we look at these traits through the leadership lens, there are pros and cons to having this personality style. Although they can be firm in their convictions and tend to be immovable when it comes to their principles, they often struggle with or are highly resistant to change, flexibility, or creative solutions that veer too far from the beaten and proven path.

This tendency to be overly cautious can hinder innovation or create environments of distrust related to others' autonomy. When mature, rock personalities can serve as a calming agent, embodying stability in chaos and during uncertain times, allowing others to lean on them.

Dear Rock Leader, are you "skipping" in your leadership style? Intentionally using timing and wisdom? Or are you throwing it and leading with raw, unchecked authority and hubris?

The Chameleon, Paper!

Paper fortune https://www.youtube.com/watch?v=TfcFrhwt17I

When I think of paper, I think of origami or the childhood game I often remember called "fortune teller." It reminds me of how it can be folded into many different shapes if you are intentional about how you fold it. Otherwise, once it's torn, it becomes a bit more unstable in its use. However, there are different kinds of paper, and they can't all be used for the same purposes. Paper, by design, is flexible, but not all paper is meant to be folded. Others serve as the foundation for blueprints, contracts, or sacred texts. And others, like cardstock or parchment, will tear if forced into a fold they weren't meant to hold.

This same principle holds true for leaders who naturally embody paper traits. Too often, adaptive and empathetic leaders are expected to bend and seemingly accommodate every situation that arises.

However, that type of flexibility becomes dangerous when it's not aligned with the Paper's original leadership design. A Paper leader who is young and inexperienced may try to fold into someone else's leadership style; a mentor, a parent, a manager, and in doing so, they tear down under pressure because they aren't "that" type of leader.

Paper is rarely associated with the idea of strength, but its innate traits remind us of its flexibility and ability to mold itself around other items. In leadership, these personality types are normally highly communicative and relational, often being able to soften tension and bring teams together. However, they may yield too easily for the sake of peace, rather than stand on their convictions. They can also be very creative and can find process-oriented ways to address problems, but this creativity has its blind spots. They can easily become overthinkers, straddling the fence of being paralyzed by so many possibilities and overcomplicating solutions because of the depth of their thoughts.

Paper leaders are usually very emotionally intelligent people and highly observant of nuance, keeping context in perspective. This allows them to be very adaptable and almost have a sixth sense of knowing what people want/need. Though if not careful, this adaptability can be seen as a lack of original structure and could devolve into being vague or inconsistent. Paper's strength isn't just in how much it can fold; it's in knowing when to fold, when to hold, and when to create structure through design.

Dear Paper Leader, Paper was never meant to absorb every pressure placed upon it. Some forces are meant to be wrapped, others to be resisted, and some are named clearly instead of quietly endured. Your strength is not in how much you can accommodate, but in knowing when to hold your shape long enough to become a foundation for others.

So, ask yourself: are you creating clarity or confusion through over-accommodation? Are you choosing peace at the cost of purpose, or alignment at the cost of comfort?

The Sharp Scissor!

By reading up to this point, you can probably guess where I'm going with this one. Scissors have one use and only one use, and that is to cut! Every pair of scissors, even a dull pair, can cut, but not every pair cuts clean. It's the simple idea that a leader is most effective when they are rested, renewed, "sharp!" When scissors are dull, they still move forward, but they tear more than they cut.

Essentially, operating with urgency but without awareness, they can become forceful and lack precision, leaving more jagged edges and damage than they intended. But we know that sharpened scissors cut with clarity and precision. They only remove what's necessary while preserving the things that truly matter. These types of leaders, when mature, are decisive, focused, and efficient, but not at the expense of people. They know how to separate comfort from purpose and ego from leadership.

A good pair of scissors is highly valued, especially when you've tolerated dull ones for so long. Scissor leaders can be quick decision-makers but sometimes can be perceived as harsh or too quick to dismiss ideas that don't immediately align with their vision. This speaks to the impatience that may come with this leadership style, especially within environments that require a high degree of collaboration, where the scissor leader may suffer from short-term focus. The scissor is also known to overstep boundaries and bulldoze slower-paced team members in group settings. Although their goal is to trim the fat, prioritizing productivity and results often comes at the expense of alienating people.

Dear Scissor Leader, whether you're dull or sharp, you can still cut. However, a dull blade damages, while a sharp blade delivers. Are your decisions cutting with care, or leaving behind scars?

There's a reason why Paper covers Rock, Scissors cut Paper, and Rock breaks Scissors, and when seen through the lens of leadership, each action represents a healthy challenge to another's strength. It's good when Paper covers Rock, because empathy and emotional intelligence help temper rigidity and make strength approachable. It's good when Scissors cut Paper, because decisive action and clarity are needed when flexibility turns to indecision or avoidance. And it's good when Rock breaks Scissors, because steadiness and principle must sometimes ground those who move too fast or cut too deep. No one style is superior to the other, but their power comes from how they sharpen, stretch, and balance each other. Great leadership doesn't come from avoiding friction, but from understanding how different traits interact to bring out each other's best. The game isn't about winning; it's about recognizing the rhythm of collaboration, challenge, and growth.

Just like the Beam Bridge, every leader doesn't need to be complex to be effective. Simplicity, when intentional, can be powerful, and history proves that. The Beam Leader moves people along by providing direction, structure, and reliability, but that alone isn't enough. Like Rock, Paper, and Scissors, each leadership style has its strengths and its limits.

You may be a Beam Leader by nature, but within you may also be the firm steadiness of a Rock, the emotional intelligence of Paper, or the discernment of Scissors. Knowing your default is only the beginning. Leading well requires knowing when to be direct, when to adapt, and when to cut through complexity with clarity. When we bring together the purposeful simplicity of a Beam with the self-awareness of these leadership archetypes, we begin building bridges that don't just connect places; they connect people to themselves, to one another, and to their purpose.

Chapter 3 – The Cantilever Bridge

The Strategic Leader

Before I go too far, let's address the elephant in this chapter and laugh at ourselves now for never knowing what a cantilever was before this moment, together. Imagine walking out on a balcony from a home or hotel that extends from the main room. The concrete or wooden base that you walk out on is a cantilever. Essentially, the "floor" of the balcony is only connected to the building at one point or on one side. That is the cantilever. Makes sense, right?

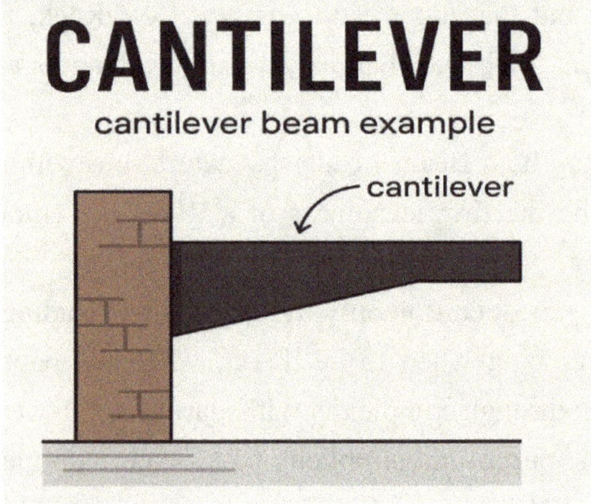

Now that's out of the way, let's talk about this bridge and leadership style. A cantilever bridge uses structures that project horizontally into space, supported on only one end. This bridge uses two or more independently balanced cantilevers to form the foundation of the structure, which eventually meet in the middle. Many outdoor balconies are cantilevered, and theater balconies may be as well. The benefits of this bridge are that it can span large distances and is ideal over very wide areas, unlike the Arch and Beam bridges, which are best used over shorter distances, respectively. Each side of this bridge is intentionally engineered to "bear its own weight while anticipating connection."

Cantilever bridge (https://www.civcon.com/portfolio/lewis-clark-bridge/)

An example of this type of bridge is the Longview "Lewis and Clark" Bridge that stretches between the Columbia River in Longview, Washington, and Rainier, Oregon. This enormous bridge is one of the longest surviving historic cantilever truss spans in the United States today, with a main span of 1,200 feet, and, at the time of its completion, was the longest cantilever truss span in the United States. To this day, this bridge continues to carry heavy traffic with numerous trucks as well in an industrial setting.

As with every other bridge that we have and will discuss throughout this book, this bridge has some "pain points" in its design and some weaknesses in its leadership style. Because the bridge's integrity relies heavily on the proper use of counterweight placement, there are visible tension points externally and unseen points internally. The tension between these points must be managed constantly for the bridge to remain upright. Additionally, the complex design of this bridge requires very precise calculations. If there is misalignment within its structure or the construction is rushed, the bridge will have gaps at various points of connection.

The cantilever bridge doesn't begin with a connection; it begins with tension. Each side extends, suspended in midair, carefully counterbalanced, often misunderstood in its unfinished form. Engineers know it looks strange at first. It looks incomplete, but they trust the design.

When the final section is laid, something remarkable happens: the bridge doesn't just reach the original target, it stretches farther than they thought possible. It supports more weight and, most astonishingly, it carries people who were never in the original blueprint — commuters, families, pilgrims, strangers who never knew the cost or complexity of what made their journey possible. This is the story of the cantilever leader. Cantilever bridges teach us that some visions must be built in parts before they can be unified. Just because people can't see your progress doesn't mean you're not building. Strategy requires tension, timing, and trust. Can you guess the traits of this type of leader? Cantilever leaders are strategists; they are rarely flashy but can be deeply thoughtful and future oriented.

They lead in spaces where vision must extend beyond immediate resources and sight. They are plan builders, always planning two or three steps ahead of most. The drawback for others is that patience and trust is required with this type of leader because the impact of their leadership is often unseen until all the pieces have come together.

Within teams, some are risk-averse, others are risk-takers, but cantilever leaders are risk assessors and mitigators. They thrive in situations where they are able to stretch themselves, motivate others, and calculate potential risks. These leaders understand the dynamic between healthy independence and interdependence. This understanding can make this leader very valuable to a team, but, as with the beam bridge leader, the cost could unintentionally create a sense of detachment by prioritizing logic over people. The best cantilever leader has these traits:

- Strategic - Thinks in terms of long, sustainable success, not just short-term wins.
- Composed - Manages visible and invisible tension within a team calmly.
- Calculated - Doesn't move impulsively; every action has an intentional purpose.
- Independent - Can function without constant support or oversight.
- Integrative - Brings together ideas, teams, and visions with precise timing.

A strong example of this kind of leadership can be seen in the body of work of former U.S. President Barack Obama. From the moment he stepped into office, President Obama took on the monumental challenge of healthcare reform, a task that had historically crushed presidents before him. Political preferences aside, the Affordable Care Act was politically costly, structurally complicated, and emotionally charged. He moved forward without the full consensus of congress or even his own democratic party, knowing he would have to withstand political pressure, media scrutiny, and public confusion — all while bearing the weight of the nation's unmet health needs. He didn't wait until the middle support was visible, but he moved forward, bearing weight independently while building toward collective change and withstanding early resistance, trusting the long arc of the vision.

Bearing your own weight

One of the most profound revelations about the cantilever is that each section must be able to bear its own weight before it can ever connect to anything else. It doesn't lean and doesn’t borrow strength from another section. An even more astounding fact in the brilliance of the cantilever is that it bears this weight while waiting... It stretches itself forward, patiently preparing to meet another force, another structure, another purpose. It holds itself in tension with faith in the unseen bridge to come.

Isn’t that the mark of a mature leader? A leader must first be willing to carry the weight of their own purpose and face their own shadows, gifts, fears, and responsibilities without expecting immediate validation or support. However, the leader must also lead with connection in mind. We don’t carry our weight to prove independence; we carry it in such a way that we can later join something bigger than ourselves without collapsing.

This requires the use of counterweights — things placed intentionally to create balance. In leadership, those counterweights might be:

- Healthy boundaries
- Disciplined time management
- Trusted accountability
- Rhythms of rest and recovery
- Emotional intelligence

- Self-awareness of purpose and capacity

Without the counterweight, the leader stretches too far, too fast, and collapses under their own ambition. But with them, they extend gracefully with confidence. Anchored and ready for attachment without needing to control it. The cantilever teaches us that bearing weight is not a sign of isolation, but a signal of readiness. It says, *"I'm strong enough to hold my part of the vision, and I'm steady enough to meet yours when the time is right."* You may feel like your leadership is suspended in midair, holding weight without applause and stretching forward with no guarantee of return. But the reach of your leadership is greater than your role, your title, or your timeline. You are building something that others will walk across long after your part is done.

Cantilever leaders stretch into places others won't go. They calculate what's possible before taking a step, and though they may seem distant at first, they are simply holding tension, not for isolation, but for alignment. Like cantilever bridges, their strength lies in their ability to anticipate the connection before it happens; seeing the ending while the story is still being written. This leadership teaches us that vision must be balanced with process, and that true progress often requires us to build patiently, knowing that everything will come together in time.

Chapter 4 -The Cable Bridge

The Transformational/ Collaborative Leader

This bridge, oh, this bridge! Bear with me as I try to be brief, but thorough in what we can glean from The Cable Bridge. There's a writing in Ecclesiastes that says, "*Two are better than one, because they have a good return for their labor: If either of them falls, one can help the other up*." There's such a quiet power in this scripture that's not just a poetic call to companionship, but serves as a blueprint for sustainable leadership. No matter how you end up in leadership or if you have the desire to become a leader, there is an expectation that leaders will sacrifice in many capacities, but it is sacrifice, nonetheless.

Living in a culture that is very individualistic in nature and action, despite countercultural messages about relationships and community building, we experience more resistance and difficulty when we attempt to create a community that requires people to operate selflessly and sacrificially, for the greater good. In my current role, I've faced some challenges around creating a culture that breeds open communication, a high degree of collaboration, and being a teammate, not just a coworker. I've gained some scars along the way, and the work to create change is steady, yet daunting.

In the world of individualism, it's easy to celebrate the "lone tower." The "strong lone wolf" is someone we probably know in our family, in our workspaces, or maybe a close friend. This is someone who is viewed as the singular figure who rises above it all, carrying the weight of the many and casting a vision to make it happen. However, at some point, even the strongest people can fall, and if they have no one to catch them, no structure of support, no relational cables tied in tension and trust, then the fall can be devastating and costly. The collateral damage can sometimes be immeasurable.

The Cable-Stayed Bridge is the meeting place between collaboration and transformation. It reminds us that transformation rarely happens in isolation. While transformational leadership often focuses on inspiring change, collaborative leadership is what makes that change *sustainable*. One empowers people to see what's possible; the other equips them to hold it together once it begins. The cables on this bridge symbolize that transformation is only as strong as the connections that sustain it.

The Cable Bridge is a modern marvel. Aesthetically pleasing and embodying the ancient truth that leadership was never designed to be carried alone, cable bridges rely on the strength given by tensioned cables that support the bridge. Together, they form a network of reciprocal trust, bearing the weight of those who cross over it. It serves as the physical embodiment of the idea that "when one falls, the other holds." This kind of leadership doesn't rise by dominating others, but it rises by elevating them. Understanding that impact doesn't depend on how much you can carry alone, but on how well you've empowered others to carry with you. So, as we study the features of this bridge, let's remember this: "Strength is not in standing tall. It is in being tethered well."

Sunshine Skyway Bridge https://www.tylin.com/work/projects/sunshine-skyway-bridge

The Sunshine Skyway Bridge. When traveling to Florida, some people think about Orlando, Disney World, Epcot, Universal Studios, and a nice Bahama Mama drink. Then, there are the people who think about landmarks like this bridge. Often referred to as "Florida's Flagship Bridge," the Sunshine Skyway Bridge is 4.1 miles long and connects Pinellas and Manatee Counties. This bridge has a long history, notably related to a tragic accident in 1980 that killed 35 people after the previous iteration of this bridge collapsed due to a freighter strike. Since then, the former Cantilever bridge has been replaced with an engineering marvel.

The current structure is more than engineering ingenuity in visible form, but it represents something stronger, safer, and more elegant. It represents a story of what happens when tragedy leads to transformation through modern design and intentional planning. This new bridge rose from a place of loss and devastation, offering not only a path forward but also a symbol of what resilient leadership can become when we learn from pressure and setbacks.

Leaders don't grow by avoiding pain, friction, or conflict; they emerge by anchoring to a new idea or a structure of trust.

Before we explore collaboration, it's worth noting that many transformational leaders are first collaborative ones. The two aren't opposite; they're complementary. Collaboration builds the trust, tension, and teamwork that make transformation possible. You can't lead people beyond form if you've never learned to walk in step with them. The Cable-Stayed Bridge teaches us that the path to transformation is suspended by collaboration.

What is Transformational Leadership?

This bridge stands as an example of what a transformational leader is and could be, but to gain a full understanding of *how* this leader operates, let's break down *what* this leader is. When you think of a transformation, what immediately comes to mind? Is it the movie "Transformers?" Is it a memory of a Rubik's Cube? Is it the visual of a caterpillar undergoing metamorphosis into a butterfly? Is it an idea of matter changing, like ice melting into water? Or is it the knowledge behind rocks being transformed by weathering and erosion into sand over thousands of years? We throw around the term "*transformational leadership*" as if it's self-explanatory but understanding the origin of how something came to be is just as essential as understanding its present state. So, if we're going to use this phrase, *transformational leadership*, let's slow down long enough to understand what it truly asks of us.

The root words are Latin. *Trans* meaning "across, beyond, or through" and *Form (formare)* meaning "to form or shape." Combining these, we find that "transform" literally means "to go beyond form" or "to shape across boundaries." Transformation is not about improving something, but it's about crossing a threshold into something new. Paired together, we begin to see the weight of these words.

The word *leadership* has softer, older roots. It comes from the Old English *lædan,* meaning "to go before to guide," and is closely related to words like *load, path,* and *journey*. Originally, to "lead" meant to show the way, to bring others along a path, often in a spiritual or moral sense, before it was ever political or organizational. In today's space, "leading" can look like many things. The rise of technology has enabled millions of people to access platforms that provide information, create spaces for belonging and intimacy, and influence and lead people toward a desired action or place.

The idea of Leadership, although prestigious and impactful, has been watered down to how many followers you have and trivialized to having a blue check next to your name or using today's hot topic to become a "thought leader" in public spaces. We seek it out for vanity, glory, and recognition. We use the opportunity to lead others as a stopgap for our insecurities, a cure for a lack of validation, and a way to address emotional dissonance and ego.

At its core, leadership isn't about visibility or hierarchy; it's simply about movement. I would argue that it's about course correction and journeying with others, not commanding them. It's not domination or the subjugation of others to your will; the focal point of being a leader is to transform the journey, experience, and lives of others we have the honor of encountering. Leadership is a privilege, not a bullet point on a resume. When we label someone as a "transformational leader," we are saying that they are someone who walks with us; we are invoking legacy, purpose, and pilgrimage.

This is someone who journeys with others across boundaries and traverses different landscapes, guiding them toward a new identity or future that they could not reach alone. This type of leader stands at the edge of creativity and innovation, staring at the old form and calling others into newness. They see the shape of what could be and patiently invest in the idea that other people can be reshaped if they experience the right environment and support.

When we look at examples of these types of leaders in history, we find that there is a pattern of arson present. Not the kind of arson that destroys things, but the kind that has a clear ignition point, but is controlled, steady. Transformational leadership is like fire, but the kind that passes from torch to torch without ever losing its heat. The fire that's used to light the way and inspire others to action and ignite movements that go beyond a moment in time. Some may even say their experience with a transformational leader is like the wind. You can't see the wind, but you can always feel its movement. You can witness its impact. That's what transformational leadership does; it moves people, even when you don't see where it began.

Does this sound familiar? It should, because we had a firsthand experience with a serial arsonist in Dr. Martin Luther King, Jr. He was more than the voice of the Civil Rights Movement; he was the tower that stood strong, despite the weather that tried to weaken its infrastructure. He was the fire that burned in the night, lighting the way for those who traveled in darkness and needed guidance. He was the wind on the backs of those who were compelled to carry his ideas, his principles, and his voice forward beyond his life and death.

Every sermon, every speech, every jailhouse letter sparked conviction, hope, and holy unrest in the hearts of those who heard him. His flame passed from soul to soul and from person to person without ever dimming. His words carried force without violence. His leadership stirred the stagnant air of silence and pushed a nation to reckon with its own breathless, broken conscience. Like the cables on a bridge, his impact was only visible in how much weight he helped others carry. Including how many communities he held in place, how many voices he elevated, how many cities he stretched toward freedom.

What is your legacy in leadership? What impact have you had on the people you've been privileged to serve? Will you be remembered for carrying the weight of others, even when you had to carry your own? Will you be described as someone who was selfless, inspiring, influential, and impactful? Or will you be known as the leader who said a lot, but did very little? A friend of mine, Pastor Jamarcia Baines, said, "If you are too big to sit under someone else's leadership, then you are too small to stand over other people," and that resonated with me deeply.

So, ask yourself this: When the weight comes, will you rise like a tower? Will your life be the structure someone else holds onto when the ground beneath them is shifting? Will your words, your choices, your conviction become the cables that help someone else cross into purpose? You may never know the names of those who walk across your leadership, but you will know that you stood, you carried, and you connected; and because of that, someone else reached the other side.

The Crossbeam

Taking a break from the bridge references, there are so many elements of leadership that we don't talk about, but I want to highlight a few that can create more discussion in your own circle of influence, and allow you to evaluate where you are on this pendulum of good vs bad leadership; potentially learning some things you may not have considered. When you think of the values, principles, and traits that make a good leader stand out, we can likely agree that there are some core characteristics, regardless of the industry in which we operate.

- Great Communicator
- Honesty and Transparency
- Integrity
- Good Decision Maker
- Adaptable

All of these are great examples and are the more widely known elements that enable leaders to be efficient and effective. But there are also some lesser-known examples that, I would argue, go overlooked or are of lesser value in our society. Leadership isn't a linear concept, nor is it clean. Often, there isn't a space for leaders to discuss their challenges without somehow putting an organization to shame or potentially throwing someone under the bus by exposing the difficulties that put them in uncomfortable or new situations. The Crossbeam is that space. It examines the inner scaffolding of leadership and the tension between what we build publicly and what we nurture privately.

We'll begin this self-exploration by walking through the differences between what's measurable and meaningful, challenging the metrics we use to define success. Then, we ask the harder question: are we leading people or simply managing power? From there, we confront our motivations in *Grabbing for Glory*, a look at how ego can disguise itself as purpose. But leadership isn't simply about correction; it's really focused on cultivation. *Guarding the Well* reminds us that healthy boundaries and self-renewal are not indulgences but necessities. Without them, we risk becoming callous leaders, hardened by friction and disconnected from empathy. That naturally leads us into the conversation of Self-Awareness, the discipline of understanding what we're leading from and how our internal state becomes the current that shapes every relationship and decision.

Finally, in Whirlpool vs. Tsunami – The Hidden Power of Influence, we explore how energy, character, and emotional rhythm define the *type* of influence we create. So, as you read through The Crossbeam, I hope you paused often, questioned freely, and were reminded that the integrity of any structure depends on the unseen strength within it.

Measurable vs Meaningful Leadership

Many people have been placed in positions of power or leadership because of their output. Societally, this is what elevates someone from just a cog in the wheel to being considered a "visionary" or "talented worker," a master of the "hard skills." It's a very visible position to be in and brings pay increases, notoriety, reputation (notability), and influence in some circles. These people are sometimes perceived as the "untouchables" of an organization or a team. To their stakeholders, they can do no wrong.

In many organizations, the spotlight tends to follow the leader who delivers results you can quantify through revenue growth, operational efficiencies, and strategic growth or expansion. They're often celebrated because they influence the bottom line, and in a result-obsessed culture, that's where perceived value lives.

In contrast, there are other leaders who lead from invisible positions. Many times, they don't carry official "leadership" titles. These are the leaders who rarely ask for or seek attention but constantly give it. These leaders don't focus on improving metrics, but they specialize in mending morale. These are the leaders who have mastered soft skills. You'll likely see an emphasis on building trust and compassionate coaching from these leaders. They have a sharp eye for culture building and can easily identify culture-killing people or processes.

They are the "go-to" person when conflict needs to be resolved or defused. This type of leader thrives in environments where they have the opportunity to develop others. You won't always see their impact in a spreadsheet or on a board full of metrics, but you'll see it in the workforce. In the employee who finally found their voice. The team that chose to stay instead of walking away. The culture that didn't collapse when it came under pressure. Influence isn't the loudest voice in the room, but its impact lasts.

The truth is, we need both. One can't survive without the other; they bring balance to the environment. There must be a healthy tension between numbers and people. So, maybe the real leaders aren't always on the stage, maybe they're the quiet ones carrying the emotional weight of the room. However, maybe it's time we start rewarding those who stabilize what others are racing to scale. Those invisible contributions are just as, and debatably more, important than the highly visible ones.

Organizations often reward what's visible and immediate (outputs), but they overlook what's vital and sustained (culture). We celebrated the architects of expansion while ignoring the engineers of empathy. In so many areas of life, the mentality we carry forward is, "This is a dog-eat-dog world." The idea that success is only attainable if you're willing to take wild risks, lose friends, damage your reputation, or step on the backs of others for recognition is one that millions of people subscribe to, knowingly and unknowingly. If we can earn the label of being a "good businessman/woman," then we tell ourselves that we are "successful."

"Bad leaders breed bad leaders." This is a statement that I've learned to be true. Not only are they bred, but they are often rewarded. If you are a leader and you punish people for respectfully disagreeing with you, then you're the problem. If you're a leader and you don't listen more than you speak, then you're the problem. If you're a leader and you demand high performance, but you don't take the time to learn what it takes to do the job, then you're the problem. If you're a leader who easily criticizes others but struggles to receive constructive criticism (unless it's positive and strokes your ego), then you're the problem.

If you're a leader and you believe you *deserve* respect because you have a title, or because you have extra letters behind your name (degrees/certifications), then you're the problem. If you're a leader and you prefer to remove people from their roles, rather than take the time to understand why they are having issues and help them develop, then you are the problem. If you're a leader who struggles with clearly communicating, but you penalize others for misunderstanding you, then guess what? If you're a leader and you experience a high rate of turnover, but you believe it's because the people don't fit the culture, then you're the problem.

If you're a leader and you're never the problem, then YOU ARE THE PROBLEM! Now, I understand you didn't want to read two paragraphs that might have hurt your feelings, but someone will read this and be able to relate to one or more of these experiences with a leader. Sadly, more people than a few will have this shared experience.

However, if we pause long enough and ask ourselves some very important questions, we will find what our true motives and priorities are.

- **To the Business Owner**: "What is your business model? Does it prioritize profits over people, or does it create a culture where people can authentically develop?"
- **To the Manager**: "What is your leadership style? Do you give respect to everyone, freely, or do you expect respect because you are the leader?"
- **To the Pastor**: "What is your ministry building? A platform that lifts your voice, or a foundation that equips people to stand on their own?"
- **To the Parent**: "When conflict arises, what do your children learn from you? Is that silence wins, and volume dominates, or that mutual respect can still lead to resolution?"

These questions are meant to be both personal and piercing, but in the best of ways. The more we can see the tension between visibility and impact in every aspect of our lives, and the pull vs. push cycles between our position and purpose, the more we can reflect not just on *who* we lead, but *why* and *how*. This can be the ground floor of your professional leadership rebuilding, but you first need to realize that the current building needs to be demolished.

History doesn't always give titles or authority to the ones who do the heavy lifting, and not every leader wears a name badge. Some of the most influential people in history were never the official "leader" in the room, but the room shifted because they were in it. Some of the most influential people in history weren't appointed to leadership positions. Power and authority can be assigned or ascribed, but influence is earned. Harriet Tubman, Mother Teresa, and Rosa Parks are notable figures who show us how notoriety shouldn't be conflated with influence. Although they are historical figures because of their contributions to cultural and national change, they were often leaders without titles. They were people who inspired changes that created generational impact through their influence, not through position-based power.

Power can make people follow orders, but influence makes people follow *you.* Power is positional, temporal, but influence is personal. Power can control people's behavior, but influence changes people's mindset. It's the realization that while power may control environments, only influence may have the ability to transform hearts, shift culture, and leave a lasting legacy.

The idea of people-focused leadership doesn't begin with a technique or strategy. It begins with motive, but motives can be blurry. You can work your fingers to the bone to meet goals and still be driven by a hunger for control or validation. At the heart of every leadership style is a motive. It's a quiet internal driver that dictates how you show up, even when no one is watching. You can have the right title, the right language, and obtain all the right results, but still be led by the wrong motives. Power-seeking leadership often comes dressed in excellence, ambition, or even service (don't be surprised), but when you peel back the layers, you discover that it's rooted in ego, fear, or insecurity. This is why it's important to ask:

1. *Am I building trust or collecting authority?*
2. *Am I lifting people or positioning myself?*

Power sounds like, "I need control to feel safe." Influence says, "I create safety by building trust." That's why motive matters more than method. You can mimic influence on the outside, but it won't last forever. Eventually, the fruit of your roots will show in how your team communicates, how decisions are made, and whether people feel free (safe enough) to be honest around you.

The bridge between power and influence is not built on skill or strategy, but on surrender and service. It's trading your ego for empathy, performance for presence, and control for connection. The real leader isn't always the loudest voice in the room. The real leader is the one who is most aware of *why* they're leading in the first place. People-focused leaders know that the true test of leadership isn't how well you can control others, but it's about how well you empower them to lead themselves. Ask Yourself:

1. *Do people feel safe agreeing with me?*
    a. Power punishes dissent, but influence welcomes dialogue.
2. *Do I measure my success by people's growth or by how much they depend on me?*
    a. Influence seeks to develop others, but power likes to hoard ability and recognition.
3. *Am I more focused on results or relationships?*
    a. Influence prioritizes both, but *never* at the expense of people.
4. *When mistakes happen, do I move toward control or curiosity?*

    a. Power enforces swift consequences, but influence slows down to lean in and learn.

5. *Would I still lead this way if there was no reward in it for me?*
    a. Power needs an audience and praise, but influence doesn't require a stage.

Grabbing for Glory

Every leader is reaching for something. Some are reaching for stars because they have grand ambitions, some are grasping for the stability of security, some are seeking power, and some are seeking the recognition of glory. The problem is not ambition itself; it is what ambition is connected to. Many leaders claim they are "people-focused," but in truth, their personal compass points towards self-gratification, personal profit, or the comfort of visibility. The irony is that even when their pursuits accidentally create positive outcomes for others, those benefits are often byproducts rather than intentional fruit.

Some leaders rise, not by lifting others, but by climbing on them. They smile as they ascend toward their goal, oblivious to the tears of those who bear the weight of their ambition. To the outside world, their success looks dazzling, but to those who have to stand underneath, it feels like a crushing weight.

Glory is addictive and intoxicating. It has a way of disguising itself as noble ambition. It whispers to the leader that their worth is measured in applause, their success is in headlines, and their influence lies within their visibility. What I've learned over the years is that a leader who craves glory rarely sees people as people. They see past people and use them as props to reach their goals. The organization becomes a stage for their play of guts and glory. The mission now becomes a backdrop, and the followers are merely serving as extras in a script written to showcase the leaders' brilliance.

What this hungry leader forgets is that those who follow are not blind. They may comply for a reason and for a season, but they eventually recognize when they are being used. When leaders chase glory, followers often feel unseen, undervalued, and expendable. What begins as admiration turns into quiet disillusionment, and trust erodes one subtle moment at a time. The impact on the team is very profound.

Instead of unity, suspicion flourishes, and instead of innovation, self-preservation takes root. People stop giving their best because they believe their efforts feed the leader's ambition rather than serve a shared mission. A culture of resentment replaces a culture of resilience, and in the end, the leader may attain their crown, but they lose the very community that was meant to share in the victory.

In contrast, a good leader does not climb on the backs of others but bends down to lift them higher. They aren't opportunistic, looking for the right time to "join the team" so they can benefit from its success. Instead of reaching for crowns, they reach for hands. They understand the value of pulling people up rather than pushing them down. Their joy is not found in being admired from a distance, but in seeing others thrive because of their being and presence.

Followers of these types of leaders sense the difference immediately. They feel valued, protected, seen, and inspired, not used. They know their contributions matter and that their leader's sacrifices are genuine. This builds loyalty, trust, and resilience, qualities that cannot be demanded but are freely given when people know they are truly cared for.

In the long run, leaders who embrace sacrifice may not always shine the brightest in the moment, but they create the strongest teams and the deepest legacies. Their influence endures because it is not built on visibility but on faithfulness. They don't leave behind wounded teammates, but empowered leaders who will carry the mission forward. True leadership is not about being seen but about bearing the burden for others. The strongest leaders embrace sacrifice, often invisible sacrifice, as their daily rhythm. Their posture is not "look at me," but "lean on me." They measure impact not in how much light shines on them, but in how much life is sustained under them.

What is the impact of glory? *Grabbing for Glory* can bring a flash of admiration and praise, but it rarely sustains long-term trust. Those who follow you will eventually discern whether they are being shepherded or showcased. Leaders who chase glory may win the spotlight for a season, but leaders who embrace sacrifice build legacies that outlast them. One path leaves a memory of personality: the other leaves a monument of impact.

Self-Reflection Questions:

1. When I strip away the language I use about my leadership, what am I truly reaching for—impact or image?
2. Do I find myself restless when I'm not noticed, or fulfilled when others succeed, even if my name is never mentioned?

3. Am I more energized by the prospect of serving people or by the idea of being celebrated for serving them?
4. If all recognition were removed, would I still lead with the same intensity and conviction?

Guarding The Well

Bridges do a lot for others and provide many things, but bridges, even strong bridges, require support and structure. Impact and influence matter greatly, but Leadership is not just about endless giving. It's about sustaining the ability to give from a place of overflow rather than emptiness. Leaders often make the mistake of conflating self-sacrifice with service, which ends up in a position of self-martyrdom, believing that their worth is measured by how much of themselves they pour out. What I've discovered, from a tiring place, is that when we lead from a place of malnourishment, we offer others the fumes of our potential. Providing droplets from an empty well rather than a steady flow of living water.

Something I had to learn was that boundaries are not barriers. I feared that if I closed myself off from people, I would somehow limit them from receiving everything I wanted to give. Realizing that boundaries aren't walls but guardrails of wisdom was one of the most liberating moments I've ever experienced. The guardrails preserve the health of what's important and sacred within us. The "open kimono" mentality, although it makes others feel they can come to you for anything, also gives the false impression to others that they *should* come to you for *everything*. Having these guardrails in place helps to protect your peace, your time, and your clarity, so we can continue showing up fully and consistently for others.

Without them, even our best intentions become contaminated by fatigue and marred by resentment or emotional fog.

True nourishment requires stillness and moments when you can step away from the noise, detach from outcomes, metrics, and performance. We all need time to reconnect with the "source" that fuels our purpose. We have to become grounded again, and proper boundaries help to ensure that our roots remain deep enough to sustain the weight of the growth we are called to carry. A nourished leader can lead with overflow and not leftovers. Your energy, wisdom, and compassion spill naturally into the spaces you will inhabit, and because you've taken the time for nourishment, your teams will feel the difference. Your family will get a consistent version of you. This is a type of stewardship that we don't talk about among leaders, but it is how we ensure that what we give to others is clean, life-giving, and sustainable.

However, when those same boundaries become rigid instead of restorative, and we begin to protect ourselves more than we allow ourselves to experience restoration, something subtle begins to shift. What once preserved our sensitivity begins to harden, and over time, the leader becomes guarded instead of grounded. Resilient, yes, but unreachable to others. This we know to be a callous, formed through friction and

Nourishment and Callouses

Leadership is not just about giving — it's about sustaining the ability to give When we pour into others from a place of nourishment, what we offer is the overflow of our own wellness rather than what little remains in a depleted cistern. Boundaries allow us to rest and refill, making this overflow possible. But repeatedly protecting ourselves from strain and stress without seeking true restoration can create a hardened layer of self-preservation – a callous that diminishes our sensitivity. In striving to remain unbothered, we risk becoming unmoved.

Examine where friction has led you to feel distant.

sustained by continuous, repetitive pressure, strain, and stress, until the skin hardens to protect what's beneath. In the body, this is a natural defense, but in leadership, it becomes a quiet threat to everyone.

A callous leader may appear strong, composed, and unbothered, but beneath the surface, they've lost their ability to *feel*. Empathy becomes inconvenient and villainized, compassion feels risky, and connection becomes transactional, only necessary when it benefits them. They stop noticing the emotional bruises within their teams because they no longer notice their own. How we lead others reflects how we lead ourselves; just as we care for others, we also show how we care for ourselves (or should).

This level of self-awareness is what prevents protection from turning into emotional paralysis. It allows a leader to ask, "*Am I leading from healing or from hardness*?" Without that reflection, the very layer meant to shield us from harm can end up separating us from the people who make leadership meaningful. Every leader carries unseen motives, wounds, and desires beneath the surface of their decisions. None of which are inherently bad, but the challenge is not whether these internal forces exist, but whether we're aware of them. Self-awareness is not a luxury in leadership; it is a requirement for stewardship. Without it, power becomes unpredictable, and intentions become distorted.

A leader lacking self-awareness is like a builder who refuses to check the foundation of their house before building on it. It is learning to observe not only what we do, but why we do it, and this won't be a comfortable ride. It requires us to examine whether our drive is fueled by conviction or insecurity, or if our ambition is rooted in purpose or performance. Without this type of reflection and introspection, even noble goals can become self-serving instruments of applause, and we end up using people to meet needs they were never meant to fill. This is an area where many people struggle, even those outside of leadership.

However, leaders who cultivate self-awareness muscles lead from alignment and proactivity, not reaction. They understand their own triggers, can name their biases, and clearly own their tendencies, positive and negative. This gives them power over themselves, not over people. Mastering self and understanding our own patterns allows us to remain steady when others sway and courageous when retreating is an easier option. Self-awareness turns influence into something sacred. Whether that influence heals or harms depends entirely on what's happening within the leader. Just as water takes the shape of its container, influence takes the shape of the leader's inner life. A turbulent heart produces a tsunami, but a centered, more intentional approach creates a whirlpool.

A catalyst to leadership is influence and the impact you have on those you lead. Like a bridge spanning the waters beneath it, leadership does not exist apart from the currents it crosses. Every bridge interacts with what flows below, sometimes calming it, sometimes redirecting it, and sometimes amplifying its force.

Influence and control work the same way. They move through people like water moves through terrain. When stewarded with intention, influence forms steady currents that draw people toward trust. When driven by ego, fear, or unchecked authority, that same force can swell into something destructive. This is where the distinction becomes clear: influence behaves like a whirlpool, while control moves like a tsunami.

Influence and control don't just feel different; they move differently. Control is like a tsunami. It's massive and loud, and even though you may have early warning of its approach, it will not change the impact that it has. It overtakes everything in its path, often without warning. It's impressive from a distance and destructive up close. People move because they must, not because they trust what's coming. Tsunami leadership changes the environment, but it leaves debris behind with immeasurable collateral damage. It may appear powerful, but its force is usually unsustainable, erratic, and driven by external conditions like ego, insecurity, or unprocessed frustration. What does a tsunami look like? How do I know if I'm one of these types of leaders?

Unpredictable Timing- A tsunami doesn't give notice. One moment, the water is calm, and the next it rushes ashore. You don't prepare for a tsunami; you *survive* it. Power-based leaders often create the same environment. Their decisions feel sudden, emotional, and disconnected from reality, and lack consideration.

- They praise you one day and criticize you the next.
- They make sweeping changes with no discussion or clarity.
- Their presence becomes a source of tension, not guidance.

Under this kind of leadership, people walk on eggshells. Not because they're unwilling, but because they're unsure. Unpredictability may make you be feared, but it will never make you trusted, and without trust, there is no true leadership. It only leaves control.

Short Duration/No Long-Term Investment- Tsunamis are powerful, but fleeting. They leave behind evidence of their impact. On its face, that sounds harmless, but it's always destruction, displacement, and disorientation left in its wake, but they don't stay to rebuild. The same is true of power-driven leaders. They may deliver big energy, quick decisions, and instant visibility. They might "shake things up" for a season, but they don't stay. They don't dig roots. They don't invest in what happens after the noise dies down. Control can move people fast, but it can't carry them far.

Power-based leaders often confuse intensity with sustainability. They believe that a big moment, a passionate speech, a sweeping change, or a major disciplinary action will carry the same weight as long-term consistency. And for a while, it might. It may even create short-term compliance, but when the storm passes, so does the momentum. What's left is a team that's often exhausted, disoriented, and unsure of what direction to move in next. Without consistency, people don't know where they stand, and without clarity, they don't know how to contribute. The result is a culture where people perform just enough to avoid a wave, but never fully step into their potential.

Destructive Force- Tsunamis don't just move water; they uproot lives, clear out homes, communities, and everything people once relied on. Power-based leaders often destroy more than they think:

- Confidence
- Communication
- Creativity
- Team unity
- Personal initiative

Their leadership is not a shared journey; many would say it's an unpredictable ride. People stop bringing new ideas, and they start withholding honesty. Not because it wouldn't be valued, but because they don't feel safe to contribute. It feels like a culture where they are only obligated to comply. They lead from a place of unhealed trauma, fear of irrelevance, or an unchecked need to feel significant. Leading with vision isn't their motive. They lead from reputation management, visibility, and validation needs. They don't seek impact; they really seek control.

Over time, this creates a culture of silence and survival, not growth and collaboration. The leader may still be talking, but no one is *following* anymore. They're just enduring and tolerating now. They roll their eyes when the leader speaks or agrees to avoid any further communication. In this type of environment, it's a question of *when,* not *if,* they will leave the team. Tsunami leaders don't build bridges. They wash them out. Their impact is real, but often remembered with a sense of relief when it's over, because no one wants to live in crisis forever.

In contrast, influence is a whirlpool. It may not grab your attention immediately. You could walk by it and not think twice, until you get close enough to feel its pull. It draws you slowly, consistently, and with surprising strength. The deeper you go, the stronger it becomes. It doesn't force you; it just surrounds you. It doesn't just change direction. Influence doesn't require volume. Whirlpools have very distinct characteristics and traits that differentiate them from every other version of a "current."

Centered Gravity- They draw everything to the core. Think about the most impactful mentor, teacher, or leader you've ever had. Not the one who yelled loudest, enforced the most rules, or held the highest title, but the one whose presence changed you. They may not have stood at the front of the room. They may not have demanded attention, but something about the way they moved, listened, and carried themselves pulled you in. That's centered gravity! It's the invisible force that exists when someone lives so fully from their values, purpose, and integrity that others naturally gravitate toward them. They don't coerce. They don't chase. They just *are.* They are deeply rooted, and they become magnetic.

That's the mark of influence. It doesn't demand movement, but it invites alignment and provides direction. It doesn't need the room, but it reshapes the atmosphere of it. Influence doesn't need thunder and lightning to be effective, but once you've encountered it, you can't unfeel it. That's the kind of leader people remember. Not the one who caused a splash, but the one whose presence changed your internal compass and direction.

Consistent Behavior- The strength of a whirlpool isn't in its flash; it's in its rhythm. It's a daily and intentional presence. Moment after moment, it turns into a steady, reliable, unchanging force, even if the environment shifts around it. Influential leaders aren't the same, and they're predictable, but in the best of ways. Their teams, students, or children know what they'll get when that person walks into the room. Not in terms of performance, but personality and presence. They don't display wild mood swings. They don't often lead with emotion one day and become indifferent the next. Their consistency creates psychological and emotional safety.

I believe it's safe to say that we've all had a leader or mentor whose strength came from the simple act of showing up the same way, every time.

- Firm, but fair
- Honest, but kind (not the same as "nice")
- Present even when it wasn't convenient for them

Influence doesn't need theatrics or performative behavior; it just needs trust over time. In many cases, people won't follow someone they can't predict, and they won't trust someone who is only safe on the good days. Consistency may not be celebrated, but in leadership, it's often the greatest form of credibility.

Inner Substance- The real power of a whirlpool is below the surface. At first glance, it might seem like nothing but a ripple or a swirl that makes people curious; it draws them in. But as you move closer, you realize its force isn't in what is shown, but in what it holds. This is what separates influence from charisma, a whirlpool from white water rapids. Charisma can be loud and demands attention, but substance is rooted, foundational, and often overlooked.

Influential leaders don't just perform well, but they carry the weight well. They've done so much inner work that they are able to handle the problems and doubts of others gracefully. They've wrestled with themselves, with other leaders, with teammates, and maybe even with God Himself. They know their values, and they stick to them. Their identity isn't outsourced to public opinion or productivity. It's anchored in principle. Their inner depth allows them to guide others through crisis, because they themselves aren't fragile in the storm.

Whirlpool leaders are the ones we look back on years later and say: "I didn't realize at the time how much they shaped me, but they did." Because real influence doesn't always announce itself, it just keeps drawing you back to the center.

So, the questions to reflect on become:

- *Are people moving because of your force... or your presence?*
- *Are you pushing them with pressure, or drawing them with purpose?*
- *Do people feel drawn to follow you, or pushed to obey you?*
- *Is your leadership shaping culture or shaking it?*
- *Are you creating trust, or just commanding results?*

Identity Anchors

Every leader wrestles with the tension between belonging and becoming. We all want to be seen, valued, and connected, but when we don't know who we are, we'll trade authenticity for approval and applause. A leader without a solid foundation rooted in authentic identity will always build from instability, no matter how impressive the structure appears on the surface. They begin to shape-shift, mirroring the language, style, or behavior of whoever seems the most powerful in the room. On the surface, it looks like adaptability, but if we're honest, it's often time insecurity dressed as situational alignment.

Identity is the anchor beneath the waves in the ocean of leadership. It keeps us grounded when the tides shift, and expectations pull us in opposite directions. Without it, we become swept away by the opinions, demands, and validation of others. We start managing impressions instead of leading with integrity. Merriam Webster defines Identity as "the distinguishing character or personality of an in-

> People who lack identity gravitate towards conformity, because it looks like acceptance.
>
> – Johnathan Williams

dividual," and living in a culture where there is so much conformity to social norms and trends, it's hard to find people with original thought, intentional impact, and a non-carbon-copied identity.

Leaders who lack identity mistake visibility for value and, in turn, they prioritize titles to prove their worth, surround themselves with echo chambers, and measure themselves by how they compare to others, not by how they're called. Eventually, this façade leads to exhaustion, because no matter how fast you run, you can't outpace the emptiness of not knowing who you are. True identity isn't discovered during the performance; it's revealed in the evidence of your impact after you've left the room. It's the deep knowing of what defines you when no one is watching, and nothing is performing for approval. I'm talking about the conviction that your leadership isn't borrowed from those around you.

Think about how much confidence you have when you understand the inner workings of something you've put together. The satisfaction you have when you pass your test with 100% of the answers correct because you consumed all the material and can explain and teach it to others. This is the freedom we should aim to have around our identity. When a leader is grounded, they move differently. There is a quiet steadiness in how they show up. They don't show up to prove something or to perform and posture, but they are simply *present*. This steadiness creates trust, even when unspoken. People are drawn to those who are consistent, not because they're perfect, but because their character is predictable. Their words carry weight because their presence carries truth.

One of the many abilities that a leader has is the ability to grow and empower others. When a leader knows who they are, they don't lead to be followed; they lead to be mirrored. That piercing authenticity gives others permission to bring their full selves to the table. It's that contagious confidence that breaks up the hollow ground of a world obsessed with image. A grounded leader becomes a living invitation for others to drop their masks and show up unburdened by others' expectations.

Identity doesn't just strengthen credibility, it sustains it. When our leadership is rooted in authenticity, even our mistakes become teaching moments rather than disqualifiers. They become bullets on a resume that tell the story of resilience, not failure. People trust and value what's real, and nothing is more magnetic than a leader who can be strong and sincere, as well as compassionate and understanding. Their presence is like oxygen in a room filled with pretense.

In the end, identity is not about knowing your title; it's about knowing your truth and who you are, and when that truth is secure, leadership shifts from striving to serving. These leaders who lead from a secure identity don't build a following; they build foundations for others to continue building on long after they are gone.

Every bridge depends on its crossbeam, and the same is true for leaders. The titles, strategies, and achievements may draw attention, but it's the internal framework that determines whether we stand or collapse under pressure. The Crossbeam is where character meets calling, where ego gives way to endurance, and where identity, awareness, and humility are tested in silence long before they're displayed in public.

The leaders who last are not those who lead the loudest, but those who are most deeply anchored in purpose, in truth, and in who they are when no one is watching. The Crossbeam reminds us that before we can build outward, we must be built inward. So, as we move into the next chapter, carry this truth with you: leadership isn't sustained by charisma or credentials, but by the strength within, which is the crossbeam that holds everything together when the wind starts to shake the bridge.

Chapter 5 – The Suspension Bridge

The Visionary Leader

Life teaches us many lessons. One of the most valuable things that I've learned is that visionary leadership isn't loud, but it is long-suffering and longstanding. Some people may think being labeled a visionary provides credibility, but if you aren't built for the long game, you'll quickly discover that the "visionary" carries a poetically painful burden. Visionaries may see the final form of an idea and will work to create the pathway to it, but may never experience it for themselves. These leaders are built through experience, not created on a whim. Their long suffering is admirable, to say the least, but their ability to endure is what gives them a strong foundation.

Their vision isn't short-sighted or narrow. It stretches across seasons of doubt, disappointment, and delay. It asks you to believe in something that doesn't yet exist, and then to keep building even when no one else sees it. When I started The Well Group, there were no guarantees or proven formulas. No promise that the vision I saw would ever take form. Even so, I felt the tension immediately; the pull between what I *saw* in my head and the reality in front of me. There were moments when I wondered if I was building a business or just holding stress and ideas that no one else could feel or see. Holding on to a pipe dream.

Yet, here I am. Four years later, with money spent, infrastructure laid, and teams built to achieve the goals I had hoped for. I can now say that I own and operate a business built on the principles of my leadership style, which prioritizes the experience of the people, not profits. And when compared to other small businesses within the same industry, we have been very successful in a highly competitive landscape. I can also say that I have experienced setbacks, missed deadlines, team conflict, communication issues, and coaching opportunities that not only grew me personally, but also changed the way I viewed business and reevaluated my business boundaries. I can now see the connection points between my business, my career, and this book. The connector is my passion for people and their success.

Writing this book has felt the same way. *Bridges* isn't just a leadership book; it's a vision I've been carrying, often in silence. I didn't write it for applause or visibility. I wrote it because I believe there are leaders who are quiet, faithful, and often overlooked. They are the ones who are carrying weight without recognition, building connections across difficult terrain, team dysfunction, personal insecurities, and organizational resistance. Oftentimes learning the lessons of wisdom that don't live in the marketplace. Nevertheless, this is the life of a suspension bridge-style leader, a Visionary Leader. We can anchor deeply in conviction on one end, stretch into the unknown on the other, and hang in the tension between what is and what could be. The "what-if" scenarios are the things that either give us hope or create what feels like an overwhelming paralysis in thought and deed.

Surprisingly, visionary leaders are often misunderstood, which is a reality this leader may have to accept. They are the ones who have the ideas that feel impossible...at first. They speak in a language that seems ahead of its time. When you come across one of these people outside, you may call them a daydreamer, an idealist, or even unrealistic, but not because their ideas lack substance, but because they require so much faith, so much belief, and so much blind agreement that it makes it hard to grasp immediately. These leaders can see farther than others are willing to look and build for people who haven't arrived yet, but this leadership style comes at a cost.

The Price You Pay

You may ask, "What is the price?"; Well, I'm glad you asked.

1. **Patience**, which is the cost` of waiting on what hasn't yet formed. Visionary leaders are often walking ahead of the evidence. Evidence that shows that the vision will and can be fruitful. Silently carrying clarity long before anyone can see confirmation. This means they must show up serving others and build even when momentum is slow, doubt is strong, and outcomes are invisible. And the leader's reward? Well, it's delayed. Their validation? Rare. And yet, they remain faithful to the unseen because they trust what's unfolding.
2. **Loneliness**, which is the cost of walking ahead of people who haven't caught the vision yet. There is no applause. When you're leading with vision, you often see things no one else can see, and because they can't see it, they don't always understand you. Misunderstanding can lead to isolation, which is a path to loneliness. You're surrounded by people but carrying something invisible; something only you were made to carry. This kind of loneliness isn't about proximity or being unloved. It's about being unmatched in perspective.
3. **Misunderstanding**, which is the cost of seeing ahead so far that others can't see anything. The problem with carrying a vision is that vision asks you to speak about what isn't real yet. That kind of clarity can feel threatening to people still living in what's familiar. The confidence of assuredness can look like arrogance to someone who lacks direction in their life. So instead of joining you, they label you "Too ambitious, too intense, too forward-thinking; too much." Nevertheless, this leadership style requires thick skin and a tender

heart to keep casting the vision, even when it's met with silence, doubt, or skepticism.

4. **Emotional Bandwidth**, or lack thereof, is the cost of carrying two worlds at once. Visionary leaders stand in the space between what is and what could be. They are both present and, in a sense, prophetic. They manage current challenges while holding future plans, and that can be heavy. The emotional toll is real, but often unseen. They must absorb the fear of others, calm resistance, and still model belief in the process, even when they are unsure of the process themselves.
5. **Time & Trust** is also the cost of building something that exists in the moment and will likely outlive you. Vision isn't rushed. It slowly takes root and grows in layers. This leadership is a slow burn, not a quick win. You must be willing to put in years of work before results become visible, and that kind of leadership only survives if you are trusted. Trusted by others and by yourself to stay the course, even when all signs say, "you should give up now."
6. **Ego**. Sacrificing your name and credibility for the sake of building something you may never be able to take the credit for. The most dangerous temptation in visionary leadership is to make the vision about *you!* Vision that truly serves people will likely outgrow and outlast you, and if you've done your job well enough, others will benefit from your work without ever knowing your name. That's not failure, that's faithfulness! Visionary leaders must lead with open hands and anchored humility.

These things, plus more, are the cost of vision. It requires patience to wait for what others haven't seen. It demands the loneliness of walking ahead, mostly alone, without applause. It brings the weight of misunderstanding, where clarity becomes controversy. It stretches your emotional bandwidth, asking you to live in the present and the future. It requires the slow, faithful work of time and trust, long before any evidence is presented. And perhaps, hardest of all, it confronts your ego, asking you to build something that may bless others more than it ever benefits you.

Although it sounds painstaking and grueling, and there are times when it is, these are the things that make visionary leadership sacred. Visionaries don't just manage what is; they carry what is to come and live in the tension of the future, stretching toward possibility, and preparing paths where none currently exist. Just like a suspension bridge, they are not the destination; they are the structure that carries others there. They bear the strain between what's ahead and what's behind, and in doing so, they hold the density of transformation for those not yet ready to walk alone.

The Golden Gate Bridge

When people think of suspension bridges, the Golden Gate Bridge in San Francisco is at the top of the list as one of the most iconic in the world. It is internationally recognized as one of the most prominent symbols of California. Completed in 1937, this bridge was the longest and tallest suspension bridge in the world and quickly became the standard for suspension bridge designs globally.

Golden Gate Bridge https://peimpact.com/ the-construction-of-san-franciscos-golden-gate-bridge/

The Golden Gate Bridge was built during the Great Depression, and it connects San Francisco to Marin County. It was built over the Golden Gate Strait, which is known for its powerful tides, deep waters, and frequent fog, which made the construction of the bridge even more astounding. The Strait is a turbulent and unpredictable waterway connecting the Pacific Ocean to the San Francisco Bay, and what once seemed impossible to cross became one of the most beloved bridges in the world.

What makes this suspension bridge stand out is its main cables, which are draped over tall towers and anchored to solid ground at both ends. It captures the quiet elegance and genius of architecture and engineering. There are distinct strengths and vulnerabilities in how this type of structure is engineered, and the same is true of the leaders who mirror it.

Just like the suspension bridge, the suspension-style leader is built to stretch. They operate in a tension that balances present responsibilities with the vision of the future; never omitting the emotional weight of their team while staying anchored in their own purpose. Unlike their counterparts, these leaders don't have the luxury of having constant support underneath them. They lead from above with a perspective that covers the gap between where people are and where they are called to go. Adaptability. This is the defining trait of a suspension-style leader. Their strength is not in rigidity, but in their ability to adapt, absorb, and carry weight without collapsing. And yet, even with all that tension, they stay sturdy and hold because they are well-anchored and committed to holding space for others, so they can walk safely into their own destinies.

Strengths in Architecture and Leadership:

1. Suspension bridges have dynamic flexibility. They have the remarkable ability to bend and sway without breaking during high winds or seismic activities. Rather than resisting natural forces like wind or earthquakes, suspension bridges are designed to adapt through flexibility, moving with the motion instead of crumbling because of it.
2. Suspension bridges have an amazingly efficient tension distribution. Their weight is carried in the tension it holds, not

in the compression of its makeup. Tension is more efficient for carrying loads across long distances because it allows the structure to remain flexible. Compression-based bridges, like arches and beams, require more support.

Translated into leadership, suspension leaders, like other leader types, carry the emotional, mental, and social weights of their team. But the key differentiator from other leaders is how they redistribute the pressure. Suspension leaders create systems where the pressure is distributed and not absorbed in one place. This allows others to continue forward with less strain.

In comparison, Beam and Arch leaders may provide stability, but they often lack emotional elasticity. Adaptability isn't the strongest trait for these types of leaders because when systems or people shift, they may resist change or struggle to adapt quickly. The best leaders aren't the ones who are stationary, but the ones who can shift without their foundation crumbling. Visionary leaders, like suspension bridges, are designed to endure unexpected motion, not crumble because of it.

Which leadership bridge do you most identify with, and which one is your team asking you to become?

Bridge Type	Flexibility	Structural Behavior
Arch Bridge	Low	Rigid yet stable; strength comes from below, with outward compression
Beam Bridge	Very low	Simple, direct load transfer; low flexibility

Cantilever Bridge	Moderate	Balanced tension with anchored arms; requires careful distribution
Cable Bridge	High Vertical Low Horizontal	High vertical strength; elegant, visible support from central towers
Suspension Bridge	High dynamic	Carries dynamic tension across long distances; anchored at both ends
Tied-Arch Bridge	Moderate	Self-contained system that resists internal stress with internal ties
Truss Bridge	Moderate	Distributes stress through a network of interconnected parts

You may wonder, who is an example of this leadership style? There are some obvious choices I could use to compare this bridge type to, like MLK Jr. or Nelson Mandela, but I would prefer to use an unexpected example. Fred Rogers, also known as Mister Rogers. Considering how simple his setting was, you may wonder to yourself how a children's TV show can be compared to a suspension-style leader. Mr. Rogers led generations with a deep emotional vision; he addressed the hard things that we wrestled with, even today, very gently. He absorbed public skepticism at every turn with patience and without anger. His presence was consistent, reliable, subtle, and quietly transformative if you stuck around long enough.

Mister Rogers never held a public office, nor did he lead a corporation or command a stage. Yet, his presence became a bridge for millions of people. He provided trusted guidance across rough terrain, spanning the emotional distance between children and the complicated world around them. During an era where entertainment and television were growing, Rogers chose connection instead. He believed that every child had value, every feeling had a place and deserved acknowledgement, and every moment on television was an opportunity to lead with empathy. Despite appearances, this wasn't passive kindness; it was intentional leadership.

Like a suspension bridge, Mister Rogers carried the emotional weight of others over time. He didn't even avoid the hard conversations. He faced them head-on, on behalf of others who didn't even know it would benefit them. He remained anchored and rooted in his faith, in emotional intelligence, and in his unwavering belief in the goodness of people. And while the world around him changed rapidly from war protests and racial unrest, media sensationalism, to economic uncertainty, his flexibility allowed him to bend without breaking, despite the social pressures. He held his posture and remained malleable. And in doing so, he held space for transformation. He became the bridge, stretching patiently and faithfully to bridge the gap between confusion and clarity.

Suspension bridge leaders aren't built to be flashy; they're built to be dependable and faithful. Faithful to the vision, the tension, and the people they're called to carry.

And so, the question becomes: "Will you be the one who stretches, while staying anchored, so others can walk across?"

Maybe it's the child in your home who doesn't yet have words for what they're feeling. Maybe it's the new employee who needs safety before they can find their voice. Maybe it's your congregation, your classroom, your team that's waiting for someone who won't flinch under the weight of uncertainty. You simply need to ask: "Where am I being invited to hold space for someone else's growth?"

Chapter 6 – The Tied-Arch Bridge

The Balanced Leader

Consider the tied-arch bridge: a graceful arch with a horizontal tie below, holding the ends of the arch together. This elegant design allows the bridge to carry substantial loads across moderate distances. One of the most celebrated examples in the United States is the Fort Pitt Bridge in Pittsburgh, Pennsylvania. Opened in 1959, it was the world's first computer-designed tied-arch bridge and remains an architectural landmark.

It stands as a perfect illustration of how innovation and infrastructure meet in balance. As we shift our focus to leadership, imagine this structure as a powerful metaphor: the arch rises toward possibility, the tie binds direction to discipline, and complexity meets clarity. For the transformational leader, the tied-arch model offers a blueprint.

Fort Pitt Bridge at sunrise https://www.etsy.com/listing/1217840195/fort-pitt-bridge-at-sunrise

What makes the tied-arch bridge different from the traditional arch is that it doesn't rely entirely on external foundations — it carries tension within itself. It combines the ability to stretch forward while managing current constraints. This distinction isn't just an engineering marvel; it's a leadership blueprint.

In the workplace, many leaders function like a traditional arch bridge. They are stable, grounded, and built on (supported by) the strength of what surrounds them. They need a solid team, a reliable system, or clear support beneath them to succeed. Although similar to other leadership types, tied-arch leaders are different. They're called to hold the weight internally while still reaching upward. Their strength doesn't come from external validation of perfect conditions, but it comes from balanced tension. Balancing the ability to dream while remaining disciplined in the tasks of the present, being able to stretch without snapping, and managing pressure without projecting it outward.

These leaders serve as both architects and builders and are often chosen for spaces that don't offer the ideal foundation, making them ideal metaphors for leaders who operate in unpredictable environments, fast-changing cultures, or organizations in transition. Whether you're leading a team through change or trying to shift

> ... prioritize self-awareness and what it means to have presence vs being present.

a culture, tied-arch leadership might be your shape.

A balanced leader seeks to bring about deep, long-lasting change. They don't look to simply improve the current state, but they guide the environment toward what it could become. These leaders inspire, develop, and shift culture by aligning vision with shared purpose. Personally, I align with this particular leadership style the most. There are traits, both positive and negative, that I can attest to be true.

Being passionate about long-term change and people's empowerment is a characteristic of this type of leader, and it is one of my foundational passions that hasn't changed over the years. If anything, it's become more pronounced and deep-rooted in how I interact with others, both inside and outside the workplace.

This book, Bridges, demonstrates my commitment to helping others grow and reach their full potential. This type of leader challenges the status quo while heavily leveraging collaboration as a form of accountability and empowerment for those who would not normally have a voice in a room they typically wouldn't be invited to.

However, being this type of leader and person at large doesn't come without its faults. If you've identified yourself in the traits previously mentioned, then you will likely see yourself in what's to come. On the not-so-glamorous side, this leader can sometimes be overly ambitious, despite recognizing that they may not have sufficient structural support.

We walk the fine line of neglecting the present system and reality for reaching toward the future. It's a form of unintentional disconnection because of what "*could be.*" This is where the balance comes in. This leader needs to prioritize self-awareness and what it means to *have presence* vs *being present*. Because the tied arch is held together by a visible tie-beam, these leaders value transparency, accountability, and honesty in relationships. They don't hide their tension, their flaws, or their intentions. They display and manage them openly. What makes this leader different from all the others mentioned in this book is that this leader is strong enough to hold the weight of others without hiding the weight of what they're carrying.

A Personal Touch

Everything discussed isn't just structural insight, but it's a mirror. It's how I've learned to live, lead, and grow. That growth isn't limited to executive boardrooms or project timelines, but in every meaningful relationship and role I carry. This allows me to stay sharp, creative, and honest. My personal faith journey didn't begin in a pulpit, and most of what shaped me didn't happen inside church walls. It was the slow, steady realization that leadership, the kind that reflects the heart of God, isn't about being seen. It's about being refined through experience, discipline, and service on behalf of others.

I've balanced the tension between being who I was designed to be, showing up how others needed me, and embodying inspiration in quiet, but impactful ways, such as:

- As an executive, I strive to lead with professionalism that isn't performative, but principled. I am constantly advocating for voices that aren't invited into conference rooms. The voices that carry insight but not influence. That's the job of bridge builders and bridges.
- As a husband, I've had to reframe my perception, not just seeing things from my perspective and learning that my growth isn't about perfection, but about being the version of myself that creates safety for my partner to flourish without sacrificing accountability and honesty at the same time.
- As a parent, trying to guide both a high-functioning autistic son and a bold, inquisitive daughter through a world that often forces them to conform before it lets them shine. I measure my productivity as a parent not in milestones alone, but in moments. Recognizing how I've helped my children trust their voice, love their mind, and feel safe being fully themselves.
- As a son, carrying the silent ache of fractured relationships with my own parents while still choosing to lead with empathy instead of bitterness, which isn't easy to do.

- As a friend, helping other men find language for what they feel, strength in what they carry, and brotherhood in what they've never said out loud.
- As a volunteer and servant, I choose to show up with consistency, even when recognition isn't guaranteed.

Each of these experiences is shaped by a tension that asks me to show up differently. Not louder. Not busier. Just... *authentic.*

What ties all this together isn't a title, it's the tension. The tightness of the pull. I don't carry it because I'm perfect, but I carry it because I believe in stability where there would otherwise be chaos. I carry it because I know that real leadership isn't about the applause, it's about architecture. It's about being strong enough to bear the invisible weights and choosing to carry them anyway.

"I've balanced the tension between being who I was designed to be, showing up how others needed me, and embodying inspiration in quiet, but impactful ways."

So much of this has taught me that tied-arch leadership isn't about being the strongest person in the room; it's about being the one willing to hold tension in service of something greater, for someone else to become greater. Just like the bridge, it's not the curve of the arch that makes you a leader, but it's the unseen ties of your inner life that keep everything from collapsing.

As we move forward, I want you to consider: Where in your life are you both lifting and holding? Where have you been assigned not just to lead, but to stabilize? Because that quiet resistance might be the clearest evidence that you, too, are becoming a bridge.

Chapter 7 – The Truss Bridge

The Structured Leader

Astoria-Megler Truss Bridge https://beautifuloregon.com/product/ astoria-megler-bridge-oregon-coast-photography/

The Astoria-Megler Truss Bridge stretches across the Columbia River estuary. A truss bridge is a bridge that uses a series of interconnected triangles, called a truss, to support the structure's weight and length. It is one of the most stable shapes in structural design. Each piece by itself might not look impressive, but when arranged together, they distribute tension and compression across the entire structure. The result? Massive strength with minimal material. It personifies stability through synergy. With this bridge type, there are different structural designs the builder can choose from.

To name a few, there are:

- **Pratt Truss** - Features vertical members and diagonals that slope down towards the center. The diagonal members are typically in tension under normal load, and this design was common for early metal railroad bridges.
  - Tension-Ready Leader: Effective under pressure, steady under vertical challenges; needs consistency and clarity to thrive.
- **Howe Truss** - The opposite of the Pratt, with diagonal members sloping up towards the center and primarily in compression. This design was popular for wooden bridges.
  - Stabilizing Leader: Grounded, compressive strength but needs a strong foundation and may resist change or innovation.
- **Warren Truss** - Characterized by a series of equilateral triangles or isosceles triangles, where the diagonal members alternate between tension and compression under load.
  - Balanced Strategist: Handles alternating pressures with grace; agile but needs harmony and symmetry to operate best.
- **Bowstring Truss** - Features a curved top chord that resembles an archer's bow, ideal for spanning long distances.
  - Visionary Architect: Sees far, stretches wide, blends inspiration with structure — may need more support systems to maintain consistency.
- **Burr Truss** - A combination of a traditional multiple kingpost truss and a segmented timber arch, commonly seen in historic covered bridges.

- Heritage Builder: Blends tradition with structure; often mentors or preserves culture and may resist modernization or innovation.

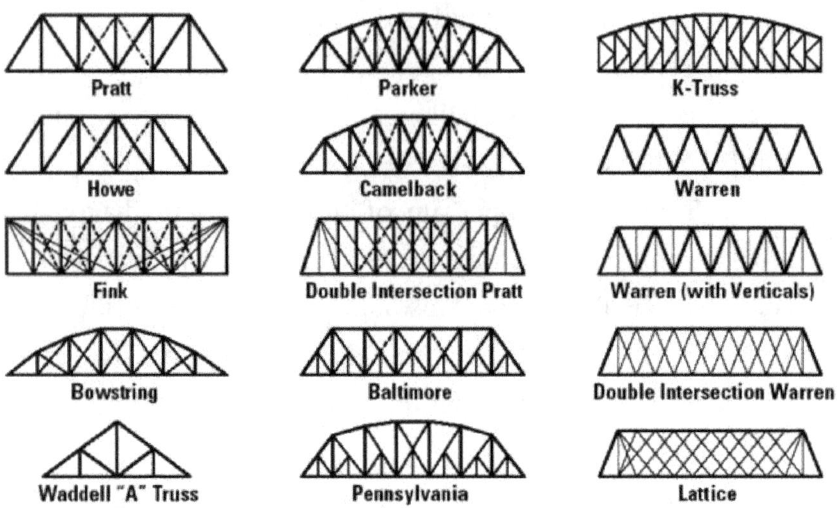

Truss bridges *https://aretestructures.com/ what-types-of-truss-bridges-are-there-which-to-select/*

The Leadership Parallel

The Structured Leader doesn't rely on charisma or visibility. Their power is in the systems they design and the clarity they create. Like the truss bridge, they hold space not by being the strongest person in the room, but by building the structure that makes everyone stronger. The problem solvers of the world. They anticipate failure points and reinforce them in advance. It's easy for them to develop frameworks so people don't have to guess what to do next. This is the mark of leadership with impact. This leader tends to think in terms of repeatable outcomes, not just heroic efforts, saving the team from disaster every week. They prevent disasters through proper risk identification and management techniques.

In my observations, there are a number of traits that this leader has that make them easily identifiable.

- Framework Oriented- Focuses on structure, systems, and long-term sustainability.
- Precision-Minded – Pays attention to alignment, timing, and fit.
- Anticipatory – Plans ahead for stress points or breakdowns and reinforces proactively.
- Connector – Builds networks of support and cross-functional teams
- Quietly Grounded – Doesn't chase the spotlight and let the framework speak for itself.
- Efficiency Driven – Maximizes output through shared load, not solo efforts.

Professionally, I work in the government consulting space, and there are always areas for improvement. One of the many cycles I work through is the procurement of services when the government solicits the services of small, medium, and large businesses. I've had the not-so-pleasurable pleasure of working from both sides of this cycle. Currently, as a prospective vendor and previously as a government stakeholder. That dual exposure has shaped how I see leadership in this space, because I have learned that failure in procurement is rarely about effort. It is almost always about structure.

In proposal and business development environments, I resist becoming the person who fixes everything at the last minute. Instead, I focus on designing systems that remove ambiguity before pressure arrives. I build clear proposal organizational structures that establish decision authority, ownership, and escalation paths so teams are not dependent on urgency or informal influence to move work forward. Writers know what is expected. Reviewers understand their role. Leaders engage intentionally rather than reactively.

This same mindset shows up in how I design reviews. Rather than relying on subjective opinion or personality-driven feedback, I implement disciplined review processes with defined criteria, timing, and outcomes. Quality becomes repeatable. Improvement becomes measurable. Teams stop guessing what "good" looks like and begin building toward it consistently.

I approach onboarding and leadership development the same way. Instead of rescuing individuals through constant intervention, I create clarity through documented expectations, boundaries, and pathways to ownership. People succeed not because I am closely involved in every decision, but because the environment has been engineered to support sound judgment and accountability.

In business development strategy, I apply structure to inform decision-making. I use clear frameworks to guide why opportunities are pursued, how resources are allocated, and when discipline requires walking away. This protects teams from burnout and prevents organizations from mistaking motion for progress. The system absorbs emotional pressure so leaders and teams can operate with clarity.

Across all of this, the principle remains the same. I am not interested in being recognized for solving problems. I am interested in building the conditions where problems are less likely to occur. Like a truss bridge, my leadership distributes load, reinforces stress points in advance, and continues to function even when I am no longer present. This is what defines "The Structured Leader."

Dr. Brené Brown! I could stop right there! When discussing intentional structures and frameworks that rely on design and clarity, she is known as a critical thought-leader in the Leadership Development world. While many leaders are celebrated for their charisma and titles, Dr. Brown has built a global platform rooted in clear structure. Specifically, the emotional frameworks that are connected to strong and repeatable structures. The invisible scaffolding that helps leaders, educators, parents, and teams move through the very real feelings of fear, shame, and uncertainty with clarity and compassion.

Dr. Brown has spent decades studying vulnerability, courage, shame, and empathy, but what makes her a Truss Bridge-style leader is not what she teaches, but *how* she teaches it. I can attest through my own studying of her teachings that her influence isn't held together by her personality, but it's supported by the systems of insight she provides. She gives people language and process tools that strengthen the unseen connections between self, others, and purpose.

What makes her impact unique is that she reaches across sectors and identities:

- Corporate leaders seeking a more authentic connection with their teams
- Educators navigating the emotional terrain of school communities
- Parents and pastors who are leading through grief, change, and healing
- Men and women who've been told to "be strong" without being shown how to process pain

Her frameworks, like the "Dare to Lead" model and the "BRAVING Inventory" for trust, are examples of how intentional structure empowers others to carry complex emotional loads. She names invisible things and gives people a mental and relational map to move forward, even in high-stakes environments.

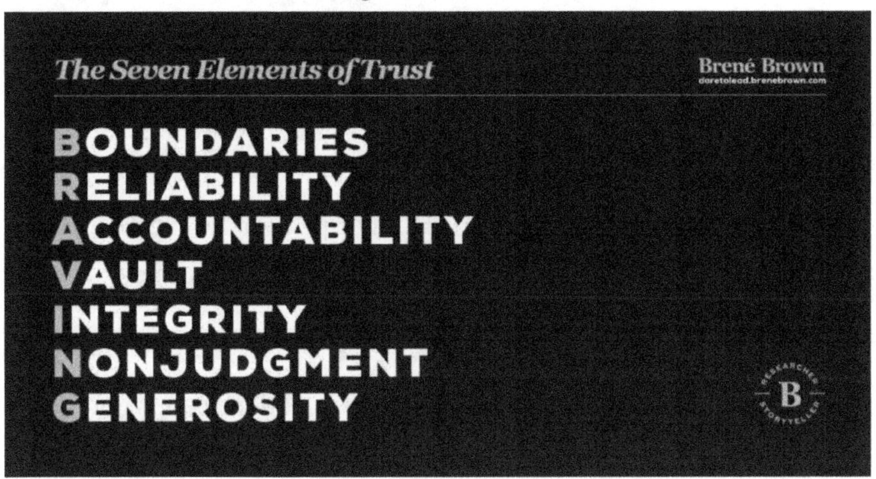

Braving Trust. Dr Brené Brown https://www.linkedin.com/pulse/braving-trust-bren%C3%A9-brown

Dr. Brown's legacy won't be measured solely by her books or her TED talks; it's embedded in the thousands of leaders she's trained and the internal strength she's helped others build. She leads by helping others stand more securely in their own spotlight. Like a truss bridge, her leadership isn't flashy, but it is what keeps things standing when emotional weights get heavy.

Becoming the Bridge

We have walked through bridges of every kind: ancient arches, steel trusses, floating suspensions, and bold cantilevers, but these were more than just structures. They were metaphors for the many ways leaders carry weight, create movement, and make connections possible.

Before we close, take a breath. Not the kind that simply pauses reading, but the kind that draws in all you've learned. Reflect on the truths that surprised you, the metaphors that mirrored your life, and the quiet moments that felt like they were written with you in mind. This was never about bridges alone. It was always about the journey they make possible, and the people who choose to take on their characteristics.

Each chapter invites you to reflect not just on the type of leader you are, but on the kind of structure you create for others and the legacy of your leadership.

1. The Arch Bridge showed us how leaders can offer quiet strength and foundational support, even when the weight they're carrying isn't their own.
2. The Beam Bridge reminds us that even simple support has purpose, and that balance does not have to be complicated to be powerful.
3. The Cantilever Bridge called us to recognize the importance of self-support, especially as we anticipate future connections and growth.
4. The Cable-Stayed Bridge taught us that leadership works best in a relationship, when tension is shared, and strength comes from interdependence.
5. The Suspension Bridge stretches our vision, reminding us that visionary leaders often hold tension between the future and the present, and they pay a price to do so.
6. The Tied-Arch Bridge pulled us into internal reflection, showing us how leaders carry tension inwardly while building transparent spaces for others to thrive.

7. And now, with the Truss Bridge, we end with a reminder that sustainable leadership is structured, distributed, and never dependent on a single beam. It is built on systems, frameworks, and the often-invisible architecture that holds people together.

If leadership is a journey, then these bridges are passageways, not destinations. They move people from stuck to security, from disconnected to seen, and from potential to purpose. However, none of it matters if the leader's own foundation isn't stable. That is where the Three P's come back into focus:

- Perception – How you see yourself, others, and the invisible weight they carry.
- Professionalism – How you show up, not just with skill, but with intention, humility, and consistency.
- Productivity – Not just what you get done, but what you build that lasts in people, systems, and legacy.

As you close this book, take time to reflect on which bridge best characterized your leadership style and what kind of path you are creating for others to cross. At the end of every day in which we lead, leadership is not about building monuments; it is about becoming the bridge and helping others walk boldly into their purpose that is waiting on the other side.

About The Author

Johnathan Williams is a leadership strategist, executive consultant, and founder of The Well Group. He has managed multimillion-dollar portfolios, advised senior leaders on risk, accountability, and organizational design, and built frameworks that translate leadership theory into operational reality.

He holds a Master of Business Administration and Management from American Continental University and a Law degree in Legal & Contract Risk Management & Compliance from Florida State University. His leadership foundation was further shaped through formal leadership training in the United States Army, where decision-making, accountability, and trust are tested under real consequence. He has also served as an Executive Member of the NAACP from 2016 to 2019, where he focused on governance, economic development, and community leadership. Across these spaces, his work has consistently bridged influence with responsibility, authority with stewardship.

Above all titles and roles, he is a man who believes leadership begins at home—and that the truest measure of leadership is not how many people follow you, but what remains standing because of you.

www.ingramcontent.com/pod-product-compliance
Lightning Source LLC
LaVergne TN
LVHW050539100826
845148LV00002B/617
9798218915711